Iwo

Effective Transnational Education Programs

Iwona Miliszewska

Effective Transnational Education Programs

Concepts, Dimensions, Perspectives

VDM Verlag Dr. Müller

Impressum/Imprint (nur für Deutschland/ only for Germany)

Bibliografische Information der Deutschen Nationalbibliothek: Die Deutsche Nationalbibliothek verzeichnet diese Publikation in der Deutschen Nationalbibliografie; detaillierte bibliografische Daten sind im Internet über http://dnb.d-nb.de abrufbar.

Alle in diesem Buch genannten Marken und Produktnamen unterliegen warenzeichen-, marken- oder patentrechtlichem Schutz bzw. sind Warenzeichen oder eingetragene Warenzeichen der jeweiligen Inhaber. Die Wiedergabe von Marken, Produktnamen, Gebrauchsnamen, Handelsnamen, Warenbezeichnungen u.s.w. in diesem Werk berechtigt auch ohne besondere Kennzeichnung nicht zu der Annahme, dass solche Namen im Sinne der Warenzeichen- und Markenschutzgesetzgebung als frei zu betrachten wären und daher von jedermann benutzt werden dürften.

Coverbild: www.purestockx.com

Verlag: VDM Verlag Dr. Müller Aktiengesellschaft & Co. KG
Dudweiler Landstr. 99, 66123 Saarbrücken, Deutschland
Telefon +49 681 9100-698, Telefax +49 681 9100-988, Email: info@vdm-verlag.de
Zugl.: Melbourne, Victoria University, Diss., 2006

Herstellung in Deutschland:
Schaltungsdienst Lange o.H.G., Berlin
Books on Demand GmbH, Norderstedt
Reha GmbH, Saarbrücken
Amazon Distribution GmbH, Leipzig
ISBN: 978-3-639-17244-7

Imprint (only for USA, GB)

Bibliographic information published by the Deutsche Nationalbibliothek: The Deutsche Nationalbibliothek lists this publication in the Deutsche Nationalbibliografie; detailed bibliographic data are available in the Internet at http://dnb.d-nb.de.

Any brand names and product names mentioned in this book are subject to trademark, brand or patent protection and are trademarks or registered trademarks of their respective holders. The use of brand names, product names, common names, trade names, product descriptions etc. even without a particular marking in this works is in no way to be construed to mean that such names may be regarded as unrestricted in respect of trademark and brand protection legislation and could thus be used by anyone.

Cover image: www.purestockx.com

Publisher:
VDM Verlag Dr. Müller Aktiengesellschaft & Co. KG
Dudweiler Landstr. 99, 66123 Saarbrücken, Germany
Phone +49 681 9100-698, Fax +49 681 9100-988, Email: info@vdm-publishing.com
Melbourne, Victoria University, Diss., 2006

Copyright © 2009 by the author and VDM Verlag Dr. Müller Aktiengesellschaft & Co. KG and licensors
All rights reserved. Saarbrücken 2009

Printed in the U.S.A.
Printed in the U.K. by (see last page)
ISBN: 978-3-639-17244-7

To Darek.

LIST OF TABLES

LIST OF FIGURES

Chapter 1

INTRODUCTION

1.1. BACKGROUND TO THE RESEARCH

Distance education is an increasingly common educational alternative as well as a key contributor to the newly competitive landscape in higher education. The distance learning market has become highly competitive, and universities are under growing pressure to develop programs that are not only current, but also relevant and responsive to market needs (Low, 1998; Marginson, 2002).

Among factors contributing to the growing popularity of distance education programs are: emergence of new technologies, growing need for new teaching and learning strategies to serve life-long learners, and political and economic pressures (Knott, 1992; Lewis & Romiszowski, 1996). Economic pressures stem from the general decline in educational funding and the subsequent requirement for universities to engage in income generating activities (Gururajan, 2002; Marginson, 2004a). Educational technologies (the Internet and World Wide Web, satellite and compressed video, etc.) have matured sufficiently to enable the development of new teaching strategies; they have also removed many of the communication barriers associated with distance education and facilitated its explosive growth (Molenda & Harris, 2001). Interest in educational innovation, methodological concerns, and desire to improve social equality and to serve individual learners are other factors of importance (Knott, 1992; Ljoså, 1992).

In recent years a particular stream of distance education called *transnational education* has become widespread (IDP Education Australia, 2000; McBurnie & Pollock, 2000; van der Vende, 2003). While there may be many definitions of transnational education, the one used in this research describes that type of education, often referred to as offshore education, *in which the learners are located in a country different from the one where the awarding institution is based* (UNESCO & Council of Europe, 2001).

Once regarded as an experimental alternative outside the mainstream university education, distance education has attained new levels of legitimacy and expansion and has grown into a higher education industry of its own (Merisotis & Phipps, 1999). This trend is also reflected in the growth of transnational education, which accounted for 1.42 million higher education students globally in 1998, of which Australia had an 8% market share (Wyatt, 2001); by 2001, the number students had reached 1.69 million (Marginson, 2004c).

1

According to Jones (2002), the demand for transnational higher education grew by 26% between 1985 and 1992; the growth is set to continue, particularly in South East Asia. It is estimated that the demand for transnational higher education in Asian countries (excluding China) will reach nearly 500,000 students by 2020 (GATE, 2000). This presents both a challenge and an opportunity especially for Australian universities, who are some of the key transnational providers in the region. The Australian Department of Education, Science and Training estimates that, already *approximately one in every four international students in the Australian education and training system is enrolled offshore* (DEST, 2005, p. 7).

Education seems to be in a constant state of evolution, and transnational education is no exception; it is supported by theory but in need of research that would address many unanswered questions. Researchers and educators agree that more research and emphasis should be placed on quality and effectiveness of transnational education programs, rather than hardware, software, and bandwidth (Nasseh, 1997). Competition for students in the transnational education arena is becoming intense. For Australia, one of the main providers of transnational education in South East Asia (IDP Education Australia, 2000; van der Vende, 2003), satisfying the needs of highest demand disciplines in the region – computing and business – is of vital importance. With the growing number of transnational education offerings, students will be able to choose more widely and will increasingly demand high quality programs. According to Moore & Kearsley (2005), this power of consumer choice will drive universities to acknowledge and respond to student needs; it will also force universities to increasingly consider the effectiveness of their educational offerings in terms of their value to students. As Chapman and Pyvis concluded:

> If universities are to attain a 'goodness of fit' between the needs of their offshore students and the resources of the university, student expectations about quality need to be taken into consideration. (Chapman & Pyvis, 2006, p. 236)

1.2. RESEARCH PROBLEM AND HYPOTHESES

The problem addressed in this research is:

How can transnational education programs be made more effective?

I argue that it is important to know the particular attributes that increase the effectiveness of distance education programs. I also propose a new conceptual model for such programs based on these attributes.

To design effective distance education programs, including transnational programs, it is important to understand factors that influence the learning process. Approaches to course design, however, usually focus on the instructional and technological aspects of teaching strategies. These approaches are based on

2

the assumption that the use of new technologies or methods of instruction alone will result in good learning, and fail to consider the factors that influence learners' responses to instruction.

Effectiveness of distance education programs is often measured by the programs' outcomes. Most of the research into the learning outcomes of students in distance education has found that they are very similar to those within the traditional classroom (Fox, 1998; Gunawardena & McIsaac, 2005; Sonner, 1999). Some authors go so far as to suggest that students in distance learning courses earn higher grades and perform better on standardised achievement tests (Gubernick & Ebeling, 1997). The main focus of the research into distance education has been on student achievement and student satisfaction. The outcomes, however, determine 'if' a program was successful, but do not determine 'why' it was successful. According to the literature, it is more important to know why a program was successful than that it met its objectives. As observed by the President of The Commonwealth of Learning, Professor Gajaraj Dhanarajan

> …it is amazing how little is known about the nature, practices, successes, failures, relevance and effectiveness of training and education delivered using distance education. (Dhanarajan, 1999, p. xiii)

Phipps and Merisotis (1999) support this view adding that more attention needs to be given to the various aspects determining the distance education context. They state that,

> ... much of the research is to ascertain how technology affects student learning and student satisfaction, many of the results seem to indicate that technology is not nearly as important as other factors, such as learning tasks, learner characteristics, student motivation, and the instructor. (Phipps & Merisotis, 1999, p. 8)

Moreover, in view of the strong growth of transnational programs in Australian universities (IDP Education Australia, 2002), there is growing interest in the experiences of students participating in the transnational programs. According to Jackson (1992) as quoted in Chapman & Pyvis (2005, p. 40), no one is in a better position to comment on these experiences than students themselves: *they are the ultimate 'insiders and experts'*; yet, *the voice of the student is conspicuously missing from research literature.*

In consideration of this need, this research study examines the issue of transnational program effectiveness from the student perspective. The study has multiple aims. The first aim is to investigate attributes that may determine the effectiveness of distance education programs in general, and transnational computing programs in particular. The second aim is to use these attributes to develop a conceptual model for effective transnational programs. The third aim is to apply the model to selected programs for validation.

To realise the aims of the study, the following hypotheses were formulated and tested:

1. Critical success attributes (of effective distance education programs) in each dimension will be evident in each targeted transnational program.
2. Some attributes will be regarded as more important to the success of transnational programs than others.
3. Additional attributes, not included in the current dimensional model, will be identified as critical to the effectiveness of transnational programs.
4. In each of the targeted programs, attributes regarded as important with respect to University instructor, will be also regarded as important with respect to local instructor.
5. For each of the targeted programs, there will be no significant difference in the level of student satisfaction with the University instructor and the local instructor.
6. There will be no significant difference in the level of student satisfaction with transnational programs offered by the same University.
7. There will be no significant difference in the level of student satisfaction with transnational programs operated by the same offshore provider.
8. Each of the targeted transnational programs will be perceived by its students as effective.
9. Transnational programs based on face-to-face delivery mode will be preferred by students to programs delivered fully online.

Responses to these hypotheses contributed to the conclusions that are presented in Chapter 5 (Section 5.4). In summary, this research made three contributions. Firstly, in terms of transnational education, it expanded on current and past transnational education research. Secondly, in terms of contributing to knowledge regarding effectiveness of transnational education programs, it introduced student perspective into the program effectiveness framework. And thirdly, by determining specific attributes of effective transnational programs, it provided information that might assist in making informed choices in the design, development, and review of transnational programs.

1.3. METHODOLOGY

Following an extensive literature search on various models and aspects of distance education, a review of the evolution of distance education and the impact of technology was carried out to provide a basis for understanding the current state of distance education. As a result, the following areas of focus with regard to this research study have been identified: teaching and learning paradigms in distance education programs, technologies and support required for implementation of these paradigms, as well as factors determining effectiveness of distance education programs. The investigation of program effectiveness explored teacher and student characteristics and practices, methods of instruction, impact of organisational support, as well as methods of evaluation and assessment.

1.3.1. Development of a Dimensional Model

Knowing the specific attributes that optimise the effectiveness of distance education programs including transnational programs is important. Literature suggests attributes influencing the quality and effectiveness of these programs, and this provided a basis for the development of a conceptual model for effective transnational programs. Firstly, these success attributes were identified: attributes relating to transnational computing programs were of particular interest. Secondly, these attributes were grouped into broader categories – dimensions – describing distinctive aspects of transnational education programs. This collection of dimensions formed a model of effective transnational programs. Thirdly, this model was applied to three transnational computing programs to determine how the multiple dimensions of the model were apparent in those programs, and if some of the individual attributes within each dimension were more important to students than others.

1.3.2. Validation of the Model

This research study employed both qualitative and quantitative methods of evaluation. The qualitative method of evaluation was chosen to complement the quantitative method as quantitative methods alone often focus on parts of the whole, leading to only isolated out-of-context and unrelated parts (Patton, 1987). Qualitative methods focus on providing description and understanding of an entire program or selected aspects of it as a whole (Firestone, 1987). This feature of qualitative evaluation was important to this study as it aimed to identify how success characteristics manifest themselves in an entire transnational program. In order to determine the influence of various program characteristics, data was collected from participating students through questionnaires and group interviews.

Questionnaires were used to allow participants to note which elements of the learning experience contributed to, or limited, their satisfaction. The collected information allowed in-depth examination of the content, structure and process of the evaluated programs (Chute, Thompson & Hancock, 1999; Wisher & Curnow, 1998). In addition, group interviews with students were used as a further mechanism for assessment. Although group interviews were more time-consuming than questionnaires, they provided an opportunity to interact with the students and clarify issues (Chute et al., 1999).

Three transnational computing programs were selected to validate the characteristics of effective transnational computing education. All three programs were delivered offshore in Hong Kong by

Australian universities. The programs operated in part-time mode for students who had previous approved tertiary qualifications. Students were normally in full-time employment, and usually studied six subjects per year – two subjects per term. In each of the programs, lecturers from Australia were responsible for the design of curriculum, detailed teaching plans, continuous and final assessment, as well as face-to-face delivery of twenty five percent of the program. Part-time local lecturers taught the remaining part of the program. All programs relied on the Internet for communication and provision of study material, e.g. subject Web sites, bulletin boards, and email. Students met with lecturers and fellow students through face-to-face sessions, and benefited from Web based support between sessions.

1.4. SIGNIFICANCE OF THIS STUDY

The provision of transnational education has grown considerably over recent years in many countries renowned as destination countries for international students, including Australia. However, research or data collection on transnational education, except research relating to distance education, has been scarce (IDP Education Australia, 2000). Research is needed to identify and debate key issues including the quality and effectiveness of transnational education programs; the results of this study may inform this identification and debate.

Understanding the education context is a prerequisite to the design of effective transnational education programs –

> whoever understands the informal yet structured, experiential yet social, character of learning – and can translate their insights into designs in the service of learning – will be the architects of tomorrow. (Wenger, 1998, p. 8)

Attributes of effective distance education programs can be identified from the literature. Investigating how these attributes are evident in specific transnational programs, and determining if some of these attributes are more important to students than others, may serve as a source of information for academics and administrators involved in planning, design and implementation of transnational programs.

1.5. DISTANCE EDUCATION TERMS AND USAGE

Distance education – the separation of student and learner in space or time, the use of educational media to unite teacher and learner and carry program content, and the provision of two-way communication between teacher, tutor, educational institution and the learner.

The term *distance education* has been used to describe the process of providing education where the instructor is distant (geographically separated) from the student (Gallagher & McCormick, 1999), or any instructional arrangement in which the teacher and learner are geographically separated to an extent that requires communication through media such as print or some other form of technology (Garrison and Shale, 1987; Keegan, 1996; Moore & Thompson, 1997, as cited in Spooner, Jordan, Algozzine, & Spooner, 1999; Perraton, 1988; Sherry, 1996). Traditionally, distance education has been also defined as instruction, through print or electronic communications media, of a learner engaged in planned learning in a place or time different from that of the teacher.

This study considers distance education delivered by a variety of means irrespective of the mode, arrangement, equipment, or software used. It should be noted that much of the literature does not differentiate between the delivery modes used in distance education and terms such as 'distance education', 'distance learning', 'open learning', and 'distributed learning' have been applied interchangeably by many different researchers to a great variety of programs, providers, audiences and media. Hence, the findings reported in the literature are sometimes difficult to interpret.

Transnational education – all programs in which students are studying in a country other than the one in which the institution providing the program is located. Australian transnational education includes a mandatory face-to-face component.

Educational program/course – a set of units/subjects, which lead to an academic qualification, for example a degree.

Satisfaction – the result of congruence between the results that students achieve and the expectations they had when starting their program.

Program effectiveness – a measure of the extent to which the distance learning program meets the participant's individual needs and that the participant would take another program with the same design (Merisotis & Phipps, 1999).

1.6. OVERVIEW OF OTHER THESIS CHAPTERS

Chapter 2 reviews literature related to distance education research in five areas related to the present study: the evolution of distance education, the impact of technology on distance education, the transnational education model, requirements of computing education at a distance, and distance education effectiveness. Chapter 3 details the methods that were used in the development and validation of the multidimensional model for transnational education programs. This includes a report on the two stages of the study: (1) identification of relevant characteristics and dimensions leading to the development of the

7

survey instrument; and (2) application of the survey to three transnational education programs and analysis of the resulting data. Chapter 4 reports on the results of a confirmatory test of the multidimensional model, and presents analyses of the collected data. Chapter 5 outlines the conclusions and limitations related to the multidimensional model, implications of the research, and recommendations for future research related to transnational education programs.

1.7. CONCLUSION

This study involved the development and validation of a new conceptual model for transnational education programs at the post-secondary level. The purpose of this study was to identify attributes of successful distance education programs and then group these attributes into broader categories – dimensions – to create a multidimensional conceptual model. Following its development, the model was applied to specific distance education programs – transnational computing programs – and validated.

Chapter 2

LITERATURE REVIEW

2.1. INTRODUCTION

This chapter provides a review of literature in five areas related to the present study: the evolution of distance education; the impact of technology on distance education; the transnational education model; requirements of computing education at a distance; and distance education effectiveness. The major section concerning the evolution of distance education (Section 2.2) discusses the history and transformation of distance education to create a framework for the sequence of events that have contributed to the distance education movements and shaped modern post-secondary distance education programs. Then, the next section (Section 2.3) explores the fundamental role that technology has played in the evolution and growth of distance education. Following on, the next section (Section 2.4) focuses on one type of distance education, which is the subject of this research study – transnational education. The next section (Section 2.5) describes the particular requirements of teaching computing programs in a transnational setting. Then, the following section (Section 2.6) links distance education with student satisfaction and effectiveness of distance education programs, especially in terms of post-secondary education. As this research study involved investigation of critical success factors in transnational education programs, the final section (Section 2.7) reviews in detail the factors that define effectiveness of distance education programs. It examines characteristics of distance education participants, technology, program design, and organisational support that contribute to program effectiveness.

2.2. EVOLUTION OF DISTANCE EDUCATION

Distance education is an increasingly common educational alternative as well as a key contributor to the newly competitive landscape in higher education. Once regarded as an experimental alternative outside the mainstream university education, distance education has attained new levels of legitimacy and expansion and has grown into a higher education industry of its own (Merisotis & Phipps, 1999).

This trend is also reflected in transnational education. According to Jones (2002), the demand for transnational higher education grew by 26% between 1985 and 1992. By 1995, globally, there were 1.3 million higher education students; that number grew to 1.42 million in 1998, and nearly 1.7 million in 2001 (Marginson, 2004c; Wyatt, 2001). The growth is set to continue, particularly in South East Asia. It is estimated that the demand for transnational higher education in Asian countries (excluding China) will reach nearly 500,000 students by 2020 (GATE, 2000).

2.2.1. Origins of distance education

Although there is no universal consensus on the origin of distance education, most researchers trace its roots to the emergence of correspondence education in the mid-nineteenth century in Europe and the United States (Mood, 1995; Matthews, 1999; Peek, 2000; Phipps & Merisotis, 1999; Ponzurick, France & Logar, 2000; Sherry, 1996). It was the English educator Sir Isaac Pitman who foresaw a need to deliver instruction to a student population that was limitless in comparison to the traditional classroom, and reach out to students in various locations (Phillips, 1998; Matthews, 1999).

In the early years, distance education was dominated by individual entrepreneurs who worked alone; later, organised formal education institutions emerged, such as Sir Isaac Pitman Correspondence Colleges in Britain, and a school in Berlin to teach language by correspondence (Holmberg, 1995; Simonson, Smaldino, Albright & Zvacek, 2000). At the same time, universities in Great Britain, such as Oxford and Cambridge, began to develop extension services. This university extension movement included not only travelling lectures, but also a system of correspondence education (Holmberg, 1995; Mood, 1995; Watkins, 1991).

In the United States, the earliest instance of distance education dates back to 1728 when an advertisement in a Boston newspaper offered weekly shorthand lessons by mail (Gilbert, 2001; Mood, 1995). The first correspondence school, the Society to Encourage Studies at Home, was founded by Anna Ticknor in Boston in 1873 (Mood, 1995). The school offered courses in six disciplines: history, science, art, literature, French, and German (Mood, 1995); it presented educational opportunities to women to study at home; communication, teaching and learning all took place using printed material sent through mail (MacKenzie & Christensen, 1971).

While initially, distance learning was envisioned as

> a way to serve students who lacked access to a complete education, whether due to insufficient resources, geographic isolation, or physical disabilities, it evolved to become a viable way to supplement programs and support innovation, rather than being merely a better-than-nothing alternative to doing without. (Weinstein, 1997, p. 24)

Neal agrees, and adds that

> these courses were intended to provide vocational training to serve the demands of growing industrial economies, but the idea of learning on one's own proved so attractive that by the early twentieth century courses in every conceivable subject were offered by colleges, universities, and proprietary institutes. (Neal, 1999, p. 40)

While some scholars identify Pitman as the initiator of correspondence education (Phillips, 1998), other researchers recognise educator William Rainey Harper as the pioneer of modern correspondence teaching

10

(Mackenzie & Christensen, 1971; Mood, 1995). Harper helped organise the Chautauqua College of Liberal Arts – the first institution to receive, in 1883, official recognition of correspondence education; from 1883 to 1891, the College was authorised to grant academic degrees to students who successfully completed work through correspondence education and summer workshops (Watkins, 1991). Harper's early efforts at providing alternatives to traditional education were ridiculed, yet he proved to be prophetic in his predictions about the future developments of correspondence learning, when he observed

> the day is coming when the work done by correspondence will be greater in amount than that done in the classrooms of our academies and colleges; when the students who shall recite by correspondence will far outnumber those who make oral recitations. (Mackenzie & Christensen, 1971, p. 7)

2.2.2. Growth in distance education programs

Following on the distance education origins described in the previous section (Section 2.2.1) is the issue of its expansion. The number of distance education programs has increased steadily from the mid-nineteenth century. For nearly two hundred years, correspondence education was the primary means of distance education delivery, but in the late 1960s distance education reached a turning point with the introduction of a multimedia approach to its delivery; in addition to print, programs were also delivered through radio, television, audio, and video materials. Since mid 1990s, distance education programs have further transitioned into computer-based formats that enable the programs to be delivered fully or in part through the Internet (Matthews, 1999; Phillips, 1998).

The most dramatic growth of distance education programs has occurred from the 1980s until the present time (Matthews, 1999). By mid 1990s, nearly 25% of the colleges and universities in the United States offered degrees and certificates exclusively through distance education programs; the number grew to almost 58% five years later (Lewis, Farris & Alexander, 1997; Matthews, 1999). In 1969, the Open University was established in the United Kingdom. This institution had a tremendous impact on distance education because it used a multi-media approach to teaching. The British Open University pioneered distance education on a massive international scale and, together with other open universities, helped raise the profile of distance education; it brought distance teaching from the peripheries closer to the centre stage of higher education (Matthews, 1999).

In Australia, in the past few decades, post-secondary education has developed an increasingly international orientation as the government encouraged universities to export their courses and import students (Marginson, 2004a; Nelson, 2003; Welch, 2002). As depicted in Table 2.2.2.a, the export of Australian education now constitutes Australia's third largest services export after tourism and transport, and is judged to be Australia's fastest growing export sector.

Table 2.2.2.a. Australian major exports of goods and services
2002-2003, 2003-2004. (AVCC, 2005, p. 12)

Major categories of Goods and Services	2002-03 ($m)	2003-04 ($m)
Crude materials, inedible, except fuels	21,466	20,739
Mineral fuels, lubricants and related materials	23,803	20,381
Food and live animals	18,399	18,158
Commodities and transactions not classified elsewhere (in the SITC)	13,117	13,700
Machinery and transport equipment	13,530	11,923
Manufactured goods classified chiefly by material	12,605	11,339
Tourism	9,434	10,212
Transportation services	7,467	7,564
Education services	4,896	5,622
Chemicals and related products, nes	5,093	5,288
Miscellaneous manufactured articles	4,413	4,267
Other business services	3,704	3,592
Miscellaneous business, professional & technical	3,170	2,985
Beverages and tobacco	2,725	2,694
Gross inward insurance premiums receivable	1,645	1,678
Computer and information services	1,091	1,128
Financial services	984	1,004

This dramatic growth in the export of Australian education is further illustrated by recent statistics showing that in the period from 1994 to 2001 the average annual growth of the onshore higher education sector was 12.8%, and the annual growth of the offshore higher education sector was 26.4% (Australian Education International, 2002). Marginson (2002) adds that Australia *has gone from a minor provider of foreign education to the third largest in the world in a decade*, and in Australia *nearly one student in five is a full-tuition-paying foreign student*.

The Australian Government's 2002 Ministerial Discussion Paper, *Higher Education at the Crossroads: An Overview Paper* (Nelson, 2002), noted that in 2000 there were 188,277 overseas students enrolled with Australian education and training providers; over 107,000 of these were undertaking higher education courses (58%). Of these higher education students, 67% of them were undertaking their courses onshore, while the other 33% were undertaking their course offshore; this proportion remained relatively unchanged in 2004, as evidenced by figures in Table 2.2.2.b.

Table 2.2.2.b. International students in Australia, by mode of study,
semester 2, 2004. (IDP Education Australia, 2004, p. 8)

	Full Degree	Study Abroad	Exchange	Other	Distance Online	Offshore on a Campus
Number	118,369	4,808	2,546	1,468	16,053	41,162
Growth[4]	11%	-2%	-10%	41%	-15%	1%
% of Total	64%	3%	1%	1%	9%	22%

In addition, a 2002 report by IDP Education Australia (2002) predicts that the demand for international education will increase four-fold from 1.8 million students in the year 2000 to 7.2 million students in

2025, and Hyam (2003) concludes that *by 2025 approximately half of all international students enrolled in Australian universities will be transnational* (p. 8).

The number of Australian universities involved in the provision of transnational education, as well as the extent of their involvement has also expanded considerably in recent years. Leask (2004) refers to this expansion as a transition from *cottage industry* to *core business*:

> Transnational education has grown rapidly from a 'cottage industry' (a few programs run for a few students by a few universities in a few locations) to 'core business' (an integral and important part of the program profiles of many Australian universities). (Leask, 2004, p. 144)

Coupled with this expansion of the transnational education 'business' has been an increase in the number of tertiary institutions in Australia who have started operating in transnational environments over recent years (Harman, 2004); currently, each of the thirty-eight universities in Australia is providing transnational education programs (Rizvi, 2004).

However, there has been a shift in perception of providing education for overseas students. The emphasis has moved from educational aid and promotion of international understanding (whereby selected students from developing countries were provided with opportunities to acquire skills and knowledge), to educational trade, with an emphasis on expanding access and, packaging and marketing higher education outside Australia (Brown & Dale, 1989, Leask, 2004; McBurnie & Ziguras, 2003). Marginson (2004a) attributes this transition from *aide to trade* to the reduction of public funding for universities and to the change of policies governing Australian higher education (p. 4). De Vita & Case (2003, p. 384) further argue that transnational education in particular is a consequence of the marketisation of higher education and *the competitive rush for international students and their money*. This view is also supported by Feast & Bretag who, commenting on the increasing financial motivation of transnational education programs, concluded:

> Distasteful as it may be to the many educators working in transnational settings who are committed to genuine cross-cultural exchange, transnational education is a multi-million dollar 'business', motivated as much by profits as by teaching and learning objectives. (Feast & Bretag, 2005, p. 64)

Matthews (2002) confirms that view and reports that international education was worth in excess of $3 billion to the Australian economy in 2001 (p. 370).

2.2.3. Forces driving distance education

The issue of growth in distance and transnational education, and its reportedly increasing economic rationale, was described in the previous section (Section 2.2.2). This section presents an overview of forces that have contributed to the expansion of distance education.

One of the major contributors to the dramatic growth of distance education is technology. Advances in technology, including computer conferencing, interactive media, digital technologies, and the Internet are transforming the world into a borderless educational arena (Bates & de los Santos, 1997; Frantz & King, 2000). The new technologies significantly increase the reach of distance provision; they enable content to be current; they allow students to interact with instructors and with each other at any time; and, they open up a global market. The technologies not only offer new and better ways of communicating at a distance, but also have the potential to reduce the fixed costs of education (Cunningham et al., 2000; Taylor, 2001). Further elaboration on the effects of technology on distance education is provided in Section 2.2.4.

In addition to advances in technology, there are several other forces driving distance education including: the arrival of Information Age, changing demographics, changing work and social patterns, declining government funding for further education, and competition in the educational market.

The transition from Industrial Age to Information Age has brought about appreciation of intellectual capital, which is now regarded as a valuable commodity. GartnerGroup (as quoted in Cunningham et al., 2000, p. 21) predicted that *by 2003, intellectual capital delivered through the leverage of knowledge management and information management will be the primary way businesses measure their value.* In addition, Cunningham et al. (2000) pointed out that the arrival of the Information Age heralded a new conception of knowledge. While previously, knowledge was of importance to an educated elite, and was applicable to a limited range of professions, its present cachet is much broader; it applies to a wide workforce, and it encompasses a variety of skills.

> A different and wider conception of knowledge as performative not content-based underpins the notion of the knowledge economy and the Information Age. 'Thinking' skills, teaming capacity, and communication skills are considered forms of knowledge. (Cunningham et al., 2000, p. 21)

Moreover, in terms of educational purposes, the conception of knowledge has shifted away from critical enquiry and personal transformation towards learning experiences where knowledge utilisation is of greatest importance. Thus, knowledge workers represent a growing proportion of today's workforce, and the value of intellectual capital drives the demand for continuing education and emphasises a shortened lifespan of knowledge (King, 1999; Cunningham et al., 2000).

The explosion of knowledge, one of the consequences of the Information Age, also promotes distance education. There is a proliferation of new information: *in the past, information doubled every ten years; now it doubles every four years* (Aslanian, 2001, p. 6). It is no longer possible to *know everything*, even about one specialised discipline, so the aim of education must be *learning to learn* (Cunningham et al., 2000). Alvin Toffler, the American futurist, redefined the aim of education even further when declaring that: *The illiterate of the 21st century will not be those who can't read and write. They will be those who can't learn, unlearn, and relearn* (Howell, Williams & Lindsay, 2004). Therefore, education can no longer be regarded as preparation for work, but rather as a lifelong effort to ensure employability rather than employment (Meister, 1998). Phipps (1998) illustrates this point by making a reference to Davis and Botkin's book 'The Monster Under the Bed'. Phipps states that:

> In an agrarian economy, education for young people between 7 and 14 was sufficient to last 40 years of a working life. The industrial economy expanded the age range of students to between 5 and 22. In the information economy, the rapid pace of technological change requires education to be updated throughout our working lives. People have to increase their learning power to sustain their earning power. Lifelong learning is the norm that is augmenting school-age education. (Phipps, 1998)

Others, including Dunn (2000), and McIsaac (1998), also point out that *the changing nature of the workforce in the Information Age* will necessitate *a continuous cycle of retraining and retooling* (Dasher-Alston & Patton, 1998, p. 12). In addition, the span of the working life is likely to extend, as retirement will be delayed until late in life, according to the predictions of Cetron & Davies (2005). In view of these changing demands on the workforce, employees and employers alike increasingly regard adequate training as a valuable commodity; for employees *the opportunity for training is becoming one of the most desirable benefits any job can offer* (Cetron & Davies, 2005, p. 43); and, employers view *employee training as a good investment* (Cetron & Davies, 2005, p. 49). As a consequence, employees are reported to be making career choices based on the opportunities provided for learning; they consider iterative training is essential to their *marketability* (Fenn, 1999). This is said to be particularly true for professions with highly mobile workforces such as consulting and IT (Cunningham et al., 2000). Thus, some of the changes underpinning the growing demand for lifelong learning *will demand short accelerated programs, well-suited for online delivery, and portfolio credentials* (Howell et al., 2004); this, in turn, will drive the growing demand for distance education.

Changing demographics are also a driving force in distance education (Ben-Jacob, 1998; Jones, 2001). High school leavers now represent only one type of tertiary student. Another type, increasingly growing in importance, is composed of adult learners, referred to by Cunningham et al. (2000) as *earner-learner*, who have paid jobs and seek postsecondary qualifications to maintain and enhance their careers, and not simply to enter the job market. Jones (2001) agrees and states that,

> there are at least three typical global higher education student profiles: one is Asian as its dominant trait; another is over 23 years of age; and, the third holds an associate-equivalent or Bachelor's degree and either has been or is about to be "downsized" from a job. (Jones, 2001, p. 109)

Jones goes on to say that these student profiles share two characteristics: they currently study technology-related courses such as engineering, health care, or computing; and, they are paying for their education themselves. In addition, the importance of lifelong learning has shifted: it can no longer be regarded as a *discretionary personal investment;* it has become an *essential personal investment as people scramble to bolster their credentials in a volatile global work place* (Jones, 2001, p. 109). Lifelong learners represent a large and rapidly growing student body and demand relevant and accessible continuing professional development programs (Carnevale, 1999; Jones, 2001).

Changing work and social patterns have also had an impact. Firstly, there has been an increase in alternative work arrangements, including flexible time and work-at-home arrangements. At the same time, the focus on *lean manufacturing,* brought about by the industrial changes in recent years, requires that employees at all levels of an organisation become more flexible and multi-skilled (Holifield & Thomas, 1999); as a consequence, the new formula for productivity and cost effectiveness reads: *fewer people, better trained equals higher productivity and cost effectiveness* (Holifield & Thomas, 1999, p. 195). This has led to greater individual responsibility and thus increasing learner autonomy (Sherry, 1996). Because of the decreasing number of employees, and increasing demands on the ones that remain in the organisation, it has become increasingly difficult for the employees to be released for training. This has sparked a trend to have educational programs delivered to companies, especially in global corporations. In Australia, the Coles Myer Institute, is an example of a corporate education model. Established in 2003, it is a partnership between Coles Myer and Deakin University. The Institute provides Coles Myer employees, located across the organisation's 2,000 plus sites throughout Australia, with integrated vocational and professional development courses, and pathways to higher education awards (Walker, 2005).

Secondly, another factor contributing to the expansion of distance education was the rising cost of living and tightening labour market: it has resulted in an increased number of two-income families. For many, sacrificing one income to return to studies is not an option. Lastly, there is an increasing need to balance academic endeavours with work and family commitments. Thus students with families and in the workforce demand programs that would fit their lifestyles; conventional time- and place-dependent education is not usually suitable for their work structure and lifestyle (Carnevale, 1999). Bates (2000) points out that such students will also particularly look for educational programs with *personally relevant content* that could be obtained through small specialised learning units:

> They will be more interested in small modules and short programs, in qualifications that can be built from small modules or courses, and in learning that can be done at home and fitted around work, family and social obligations. (Bates, 2000)

Declining funds also drive distance education opportunities. Governments are increasingly reluctant to fund growing demand for further education (Dudley, 1998), so institutions of higher education are driven towards *for profit education on a global scale* necessitated by *desperate need to improve income to compensate for the lack of public funding or budget cuts* (Gururajan, 2002). In Australia, foreign students have become crucial to the resource base of many Australian universities. International education provides more than 10% of the average revenues of Australian institutions (Marginson, 2002).

16

Consequently, universities need to attract larger number of students to reduce cost of their programs. Universities expect that students will be attracted to distance education programs, and that they will pay for the opportunity to study while not being restricted by location or time. However, while students are likely to look for this education at universities first, they will not hesitate to go to other providers if the university offerings do not meet their needs (Bates, 2000).

Competition is another driving force. The corporate world sees the potential in the educational market and challenges universities by providing alternative courses and training programs to meet the rapidly growing demand. Middlehurst (2003) identified the following categories of commercial provider and provision: corporate universities, private and for-profit providers, media and publishing businesses, and educational services and brokers.

Many corporations, especially large ones such as McDonalds, Ernst & Young, or Lufthansa, are developing corporate universities (Taylor & Paton, 2002); at present, there are more than 2000 of such initiatives worldwide (Middlehurst, 2003).

New private higher education institutions have also emerged recently on the distance education market as a result of a growing demand for foundation-level higher education (learner in the 18-25 age group), and for continuing and specialist education. These institutions usually provide specialised programs in business, engineering, information technology, and teacher training to the niche market of working adults (Middlehurst, 2003; Ryan, 2002). The University of Phoenix is one example of this type of provider.

In addition, there has been a growth in the activities of commercial companies supporting on-line infrastructure of universities including the Provincial Radio and TV Universities in China, or BBC's alliance with the Open University in the UK. Publishing companies such as Pearson and Thomson Learning, are also involved in supporting universities and other educational providers, and developing new initiatives. While universities supply learning, assessment, and accreditation services, the publishers contribute their expertise in marketing, distribution, and content and electronic delivery systems (Middlehurst, 2003).

Finally, there has been huge growth in educational brokers over the recent years (Cunningham et al., 2000). The brokers, of whom Learnerdirect in the UK is an example, mediate between learners and companies and providers; they provide learners with access to study materials through conveniently located learning centers equipped with the latest technology. Corporations are also promoting distance education course design, and course management tools (Middlehurst, 2003). Middlehurst points at the growing influence of such corporations in the distance education market, and the growing reliance of universities on this new type of provider:

> Many corporate universities rely on contractors for the development of tools, templates and expertise not available in-house and some educational service companies will offer to set up and run the corporate university for you, providing enrolment systems and facilities management services. Increasingly, as traditional universities invest in large-scale networked learning to develop 'managed learning environments', they too are becoming dependent on commercial educational service providers. (Middlehurst, 2003, p. 31)

This marketing effort further increases competition and applies additional pressure on the non-profit university sector to provide distance education opportunities (Blumenstyk, 1999).

2.2.4. Effect of technology on distance education

As indicated in the previous section (Section 2.2.3), the recent acceleration in the growth of distance education was enabled by advancements in technology. However, technology played a significant role in the development of distance education prior to the emergence of the computer and high-speed network connections; earlier technologies including print, radio, television, and video also shaped distance education and contributed to its growth.

Over the years, changes in technology generated several significant milestones that affected the distance education market in terms of scale and delivery. Having examined the milestones, Sherron & Boettcher (1997) defined four generations of distance education technologies according to five characteristics: (1) media and technologies, (2) communication features, (3) student characteristics and goals, (4) educational philosophy and curriculum design, and (5) infrastructure. This definition was further adapted by Lewis, Snow, Farris & Levin (US Department of Education, 1999), wherein the four generations of technologies were described in terms of primary characteristics, timeframe, media, and communication features as summarised in Table 2.2.4.a. The distinguishing features of the generations include:

- the type of communication involved for instance, one-way, two-way, or multiple-way communication;
- the type of the communicated information for instance, voice, video, data; and the volume of information that can be communicated that is, type of communication channels;
- and, the speed of communication.

Table 2.2.4.a. Generations of distance education technologies.
(US Department of Education, 1999, p. 4)

	First Generation	Second Generation	Third Generation	Fourth Generation
Primary Feature	Predominantly one technology	Multiple technologies without computers	Multiple technologies including computers and computer networking	Multiple technologies including the beginning of high-bandwidth computer technologies
Timeframe	1850s to 1960	1960 to 1985	1985 to 1995	1995 to 2005 (est.)
Media	• Print (1890+) • Radio (1930s) • Television (1950s and 1960s)	• Audiocassettes • Television • Videocassettes • Fax • Print	• Electronic mail, chat sessions, and bulletin boards using computers and computer networks • Computer programs and resources packaged on disks, CDs, and the Internet • Audioconferencing • Seminar and large-room videoconferencing via terrestrial, satellite, cable, and phone technologies • Fax • Print	• Electronic mail, chat sessions, and bulletin boards using computers and computer networks plus high-bandwidth transmission for individualized, customized, and live video interactive learning experiences • Computer programs and resources packaged on disks, CDs, Internet • Audioconferencing • Desktop videoconferencing via terrestrial, satellite, cable, and phone technologies • Fax • Print
Communication Features	• Primarily one-way communication • Interaction between faculty and student by telephone and mail • Occasionally supplemented by onsite facilitators and student mentors	• Primarily one-way communication • Interaction between faculty and student by telephone, fax, and mail • Occasionally supplemented by face-to-face meetings	• Significant broadband communication from faculty to students via print, computer programs, and videoconferencing • Two-way interactive capabilities enabling asynchronous and synchronous communication between faculty and students and among students • Internet good for text, graphics and video snippets	• Two-way interactive real-time capabilities of audio and video • Asynchronous and synchronous communication between faculty and students and among students • Full 30-frame-per-second digital video transmission with databases of content resources available via the Internet and World Wide Web • Lengthy digital video programming available on demand

The first generation includes the period between early to mid twentieth century when print, radio, and broadcast television prevailed. Those media involved one-way communication as information was passed from teachers to students; there was no interaction among students, and minimal interaction between students and teachers. In addition, the radio and television broadcasts were time-dependent (Sherron & Boettcher, 1997).

The advent of the VCR and cable television in the early 1960s heralded the beginning of the second generation. The milestone that distinguished the second generation from its predecessor was the removal of time dependency: the broadcast portion of a distance education program was no longer tied to predetermined times (Sherron & Boettcher, 1997). In addition, videocassettes with their stop and rewind options gave learners control over the learning material: lectures could be interrupted and reviewed (Gunawardena & McIsaac, 2005). However, this generation still afforded little interaction among students and between students and teachers.

The third generation arrived by the mid-1980s together with the personal computer and two-way videoconferencing. Two milestones separated this generation form the previous ones: one, the new technologies made it possible to communicate increasingly complex and large amounts of information to students; and two, they enabled interaction among students, and between students and teachers (US Department of Education, 1999).

This growth in technological advancements accelerated significantly during the 1990s with the use of computer-mediated learning technologies, for example two-way interactive video; two-way audio and Web-based asynchronous communication; and on-line or offline Internet Web-based instruction (Phipps & Merisotis, 1999; Ponzurick et al., 2000; Sherry, 1996; Setaro, 2000). It was also the beginning of the fourth generation. This generation signified yet another milestone namely, increased interactivity among students, between students and teachers, and between students and content thanks to high-speed networks and more sophisticated software. Consequently, the amount and types of information that could be communicated has significantly increased, and the exchange of information took significantly less time (Sherron & Boettcher, 1997).

The current landscape of distance education includes a wide spectrum of technologies, spanning all generations. Although the technologies of the first generation have been surpassed by several other generations, they continue to play a considerable role in distance education. Firstly, radio and television are a viable option in developing countries such as India and China where the infrastructure to support more recent technologies has yet to be developed (Middlehurst, 2003); and, in developed countries, radio and television is used extensively by institutions such as the British Open University to deliver programs to a large number of learners (Gunawardena & McIsaac, 2005). Secondly, print *remains a very important support medium for electronically delivered distance education* (Gunawardena & McIsaac, 2005, p. 365).

Advancements in technology have enabled a change in the learning environment from a classroom-based, teacher-centered model to a student-centered, technology-based model (Doucette, 1994; Guskin, 1994; Sanchez, 1994). Romiszowski reinforced this point by stating that:

> … the costs of telecommunications are falling whereas the costs of educational space, staffing, and transport are rising, so that over time the economical equation will favor the increased use of telecommunication-based education (Romiszowski, 1993).

However, recent developments in interactive multimedia technologies such as automated response systems and interactive multimedia on-line, which allow for individualised and collaborative learning, obscure the distinction between distance and traditional education. These technologies enable the creation of virtual communities also in traditional settings. Consequently, all interactions with teachers, course content, learning activities, assessment, and support services are delivered on-line even for campus-based students (Taylor, 2001). The use of on-line education technologies has been accompanied by the development of pedagogies to improve the merging of distance education and asynchronous learning (Cashion & Palmieri, 2002). To this end, instructional designers were employed to create online units, and tutors were employed to implement the learning programs.

Through international collaboration, students around the world can participate in cooperative learning activities sharing information through computer networks. In such cases, global classrooms may have participants from various countries interacting with each other at a distance. Many mediated educational activities allow students to participate in collaborative learning activities (Gunawardena & McIsaac, 2005). Hall (1995) even suggests that the descriptor *distance learning* is becoming less and less relevant with respect to distance programs and students. According to Hall, *connected learning* might be a more accurate descriptor, reflecting the impact that technology has had on distance education pedagogy. However, he urges a close examination of the *new relationships between pedagogies that the new technologies make feasible.*

The changes in communications and information technology have necessitated various transformations in higher education institutions. Daryl Le Grew (1995) described a *paradigm shift* by comparing what learning was like in an industrial society and what it is now in an information society; the shifts included one from 'technology peripheral' to 'multimedia central', and another from 'local-focused' to 'global networking' (Table 2.2.4.b).

Table 2.2.4.b. Paradigm shift in education. (As presented in Mak, 1999.)

Industrial Society	Information Society
Technology peripheral	Multimedia central
Once-only education	Life-long learning
Fixed curriculum	Flexible/open curriculum
Institutional focus	Learner focus
Self-contained	Partnership
Local-focused	Global networking

Although technology is a central part of many distance education programs, it is important to remember that technology is just the method of conveying some content (Huch, 1999); technology is not the focus of the learning endeavour (Langford & Hardin, 1999). While distance education is evolving and changing so rapidly that no one can accurately predict its future,

> it is clear that the market for distance education will continue to expand in the next century. However, we should be aware of the limitations of distance education, especially in its electronic manifestations, and use it appropriately. (Neal, 1999, p. 43)

According to Weinstein,

> … the human touch cannot be delivered remotely. Distance learning technologies are intended to support an integrated program, not replace it. Balancing virtual and 'real' interaction will be one of the key educational challenges as we enter the 21st century… (Weinstein, 1997, p. 25)

In short, technology *cannot replace most human contact without significant quality losses* (Merisotis & Phipps, 1999, p. 17).

In brief, this section outlined the evolution of post-secondary distance education from its inception to the present; its progression from informal programs offered by individual providers to a well organised formal educational alternative; its purpose and characteristics; its expansion and internationalisation; and, the various forces that have shaped its growth. It highlighted the crucial role that advancements in technology have played in propelling the evolution of distance education; it also noted that technology has its limitations – it can facilitate, but not replace teaching.

2.3. DISTANCE EDUCATION MODELS

As outlined in the previous section (Section 2.2), distance education has evolved considerably from the inception of the first correspondence course to this day. The evolution involved the number and types of programs offered, the technology used in their delivery, as well as the number and types of providers offering such programs. This section discusses various distance education models classified according to the above components: provider, program, and technology.

Current distance education programs represent a wide range of approaches. One end of the spectrum offers fully on-line programs relying on computer-based student contact and feedback; the other end offers technology-assisted programs with computer-delivered instruction, electronic mail communication between students and teachers, some centralised face-to-face class sessions, and weekend meetings of cluster groups. The programs have different scopes (from local to international), target a variety of audiences, are offered at various educational levels, and represent different settings (from classical universities operating at a distance to modern open and flexible institutions). Accordingly, distance education models are categorised from a number of perspectives.

2.3.1. Models based on organisational provider profile

Rumble (1986) and Holmberg (1995) identified three models determined by the organisational and administrative structures of distance education providers, sole responsibility, mixed mode, and consortium.

- Sole responsibility, of which Open University in the United Kingdom is an example, is a model where distance education is the special purpose and responsibility of the institution; all planning, funds, staff, and other resources are devoted to this purpose:

  > With the sole purpose being distance education, these institutions dedicate all their management structures to that end. All teaching and administrative activities and all funds are devoted exclusively to distance education. These institutions generally have no campus; instead, students use a system of local and regional study sites. Courses are usually designed by course teams. (GDNET, 2005)

22

- Mixed mode refers to institutions where both traditional and distance education occur, such as the Charles Sturt University, and Monash University in Australia. In mixed mode institutions, responsibility for organisation may rest with a single department within the institution, with the institution responsible for administration; or, departments may be responsible for both organisation and administration of their own programs; or, a dedicated unit within the organisation may offer distance education in a variety of disciplines and be solely devoted to this purpose. Open Learning Institute at Charles Sturt University, and Distance Education Centre at Monash University in Australia are examples of dedicated units (Fraser & Deane, 1998).

- Consortium, refers to a group of institutions devoted to distance education. In this model two or more institutions share distance learning materials or functions. For instance, one institution is responsible for producing materials, another for tutor support, or accreditation. The institutions involved may be universities (traditional, single or dual mode) or university departments, government agencies, business partners, radio, TV or media production companies. Here, students may enrol at their own institution, use centrally developed learning materials, and transfer credits to their academic records (UNESCO, 2000; Verduin & Clark, 1991). Examples of consortia in three different countries include the National Technological University in the USA, NETTUNO and CUD in Italy, and the Open Learning Agency and Contact North/Contact Nord in Canada (UNESCO, 2000).

2.3.2. Models based on provider's attitude to distance education

Fraser & Deane (1998) categorised distance education models in terms of institutional attitudes to distance education. The first model recognises distance education as a mode in its own right. The learning experience is adaptable and learner-controlled. The second model regards distance education as a substitute for conventional education. In this model, students are treated as members of a class, there is a mandatory face-to-face component, and the learning experience is paced and controlled by the institution. In addition to these two models there are many variations that partly resemble either or both of them.

2.3.3. Models determined by delivery technology

Another perspective used in categorising distance education models is one based on technologies used to support the various components of the instructional process, and the placement of control over the pace and location of instruction. In some models, the teachers and institution have primary control, as is the case in a traditional classroom environment. In others, the control rests with the student. The models identified in this categorisation are: distributed classroom, independent learning, and open learning plus class (Leach & Walker, 2000).

- Distributed classroom is a model where interactive telecommunication technologies are used to extend a program based in one location to students in one or more other locations. The control over the pace and location of instruction rests with the teachers and the institution where the program is based.
- Independent learning, sometimes referred to as flexible learning, is a model where students learn when, how, what, and where they want (Van den Brande, 1992). They are provided with a variety of educational materials for a self-paced study, and access to teachers who provide guidance, and evaluate their work. Telephone, e-mail, computer conferencing and correspondence are used as a means of communication. The presence of two-way communication distinguishes independent learning from teach-yourself programmes (Keegan, 1996).
- Open learning plus class model involves the use of course material allowing students to study independently, combined with periodical use of interactive telecommunications technologies for group meetings among all enroled students.

Taylor (2001) categorised distance education operations in terms of generations determined by the supporting technologies; first, the Correspondence model based on print technology; second, the Multimedia Model based on print, audio and video technologies; third, the Telelearning Model, based on telecommunications technologies; fourth, the Flexible Learning Model based on the Internet; and fifth, Intelligent Flexible Learning Model, a derivation of the fourth generation, capitalising further on the Internet and the Web. According to Taylor (2001), the difference between the fourth and fifth generations is in the way in which technology is used. The fifth generation extends the context of Internet-based delivery by incorporating the use of automated response systems and intelligent object databases; as a consequence tuition costs decrease and thereby stimulate economies of scale:

> A key consideration for the fifth generation is the use of automated response systems to reduce the variable cost
> of computer mediated communication (CMC) which in the fourth generation is quite resource intensive. (Taylor,
> 2000, p. 1)

Some of the characteristics of the various generations that are relevant to the quality of teaching and learning, as well as an indicator of institutional variable costs are summarised in Table 2.3.3.

Table 2.3.3. Five generations of distance education. (Taylor, 2001, p. 3)

Models of Distance Education and Associated Delivery Technologies	Characteristics of Delivery Technologies					
	Flexibility			Highly Refined Materials	Advanced Interactive Delivery	Institutional Variable Costs Approaching Zero
	Time	Place	Pace			
FIRST GENERATION The Correspondence Model						
• Print	Yes	Yes	Yes	Yes	No	No
SECOND GENERATION The Multimedia Model						
• Print	Yes	Yes	Yes	Yes	No	No
• Audiotape	Yes	Yes	Yes	Yes	No	No
• Videotape	Yes	Yes	Yes	Yes	No	No
• Computer-based learning (e.g. CML/CAI/IMM)	Yes	Yes	Yes	Yes	Yes	No
• Interactive video (disk and tape)	Yes	Yes	Yes	Yes	Yes	No
THIRD GENERATION The Telelearning Model						
• Audio tele-conferencing	No	No	No	No	Yes	No
• Video-conferencing	No	No	No	No	Yes	No
• Audiographic Communication	No	No	No	Yes	Yes	No
• Broadcast TV/Radio and audio-teleconferencing	No	No	No	Yes	Yes	No
FOURTH GENERATION The Flexible Learning Model						
• Interactive multimedia (IMM) online	Yes	Yes	Yes	Yes	Yes	Yes
• Internet-based access to WWW resources	Yes	Yes	Yes	Yes	Yes	Yes
• Computer-mediated communication	Yes	Yes	Yes	Yes	Yes	No
FIFTH GENERATION The Intelligent Flexible Learning Model						
• Interactive multimedia (IMM) online	Yes	Yes	Yes	Yes	Yes	Yes
• Internet-based access to WWW resources	Yes	Yes	Yes	Yes	Yes	Yes
• Computer-mediated communication, using automated response systems	Yes	Yes	Yes	Yes	Yes	Yes
• Campus portal access to institutional processes and resources	Yes	Yes	Yes	Yes	Yes	Yes

Related to Taylor's (2001) fourth and fifth generation models of distance education was Gallagher's (2001) categorisation of on-line education. Gallagher identified three types of on-line education, whereby the types – Web Supplemented, Web Dependent, and Fully On-line – varied with respect to their dependence on the Internet.

- Web supplemented – In this mode, online information is used to supplement traditional forms of delivery, and students' participation on-line is optional. Students can access online additional information about their programs and individual subjects; the information may include course descriptions and study guides, assessment details, reading lists, and on-line learning resources.

- Web dependent – While some traditional on-campus component is still present, in this mode, students must participate on-line in learning and communication. On-line learning involves interaction with study content; Internet is also used to communicate with staff and fellow students.

- Fully on-line – There is no traditional on-campus component in this mode and no face-to-face interaction. All interactions with study content, as well as staff and students is conducted on-line. In addition, learning activities, assessment, and support services are also delivered on-line.

Finder and Raleigh, as cited in (Meares, 2001), provided an alternative definition of the on-line models; they distinguish between four different levels based on the importance of the on-line component of a distance education program. The four levels are: informational, supplemental, essential, and fully on-line.

- Informational – the on-line component serves as an optional source of general program information, for example program outline or assignment description.

- Supplemental – the on-line component complements other forms of instruction, for example it contains lecture notes. Students are required to use the Web to complete part of their program. On-line learning materials usually include links to related secondary sources.

- Essential – the on-line unit forms an integral part of the program and students must use it to complete the program. Most learning materials are available on the Web; students use the Web to complete assignments.

- Fully On-line – the program does not include any face-to-face interaction and is delivered entirely on-line.

In conclusion, this section presented categorisations of distance education models according to the organisational and administrative structures of the providers; providers' attitudes towards distance education; and, supporting technologies.

2.4. TRANSNATIONAL MODEL OF DISTANCE EDUCATION

Following on the overview of the evolution of distance education and the associated discussion on different distance education models presented in the previous sections (Section 2.2 and 2.3), this section focuses on one particular type of distance education which is the subject of this research study – transnational education. The section reviews the definition of transnational education, its typology, factors determining demand and supply, attributes of typical transnational programs, and the importance of face-to-face interaction in those programs.

2.4.1. Transnational education – definition

The review of recent studies of transnational education revealed that there is no agreement about what to include in this category. Similarly, there is no agreement on the various sub-definitions that inform the subject. For the purpose of this research study, a working definition of transnational education produced by UNESCO and the Council of Europe for their Code of Practice in the Provision of Transnational Education was used (UNESCO & Council of Europe, 2001). This states that transnational education includes

All types of higher education study programme, or sets of courses of study, or educational services (including those of distance education) in which the learners are located in a country different from the one where the awarding institution is based. Such programmes may belong to the educational system of a State different from the State in which it operates, or may operate independently of any national system. (UNESCO & Council of Europe, 2001)

This definition includes education that is provided by collaborative arrangements, such as franchising, twinning, joint degrees where study programs are provided by another partner, as well as non-collaborative arrangements such as branch campuses, offshore institutions, and corporate universities.

The Australian Department of Education Science and Training (DEST, 2005) provides a definition of *Australian Transnational Education*; this definition includes two additional requirements:

(1) that the transnational program be delivered and/or assessed by an accredited Australian provider; and

(2) that the delivery include a face-to-face component.

It further stresses that, in contrast to distance education provided in purely distance mode, transnational education includes a physical presence of instructors offshore, either directly by the Australian provider, or indirectly through a formal agreement with a local institution:

Australian transnational education and training, also known as offshore or cross-border education and training, refers to the delivery and/or assessment of programs/courses by an accredited Australian provider in a country other than Australia, where delivery includes a face-to-face component. The education and/or training activity may lead to an Australian qualification or may be a non-award course, but in either case an accredited/approved/recognised Australian provider is associated with the education/training activity.

As distinct from education and training provided in a purely distance mode, transnational education and training includes a physical presence of instructors offshore, either directly by the Australian provider, or indirectly through a formal agreement with a local institution/organisation. (DEST, 2005, p. 6)

2.4.2. Typology of transnational education

There are a great number of different relationships between different types of transnational education providers, delivery mechanisms, and programs/awards. Charting these types is a difficult task, as the constantly evolving, highly complex situation includes an array of partnerships, consortia, articulation agreements, modes of delivery, public, private, off-shore, for-profit and corporate elements. Various models of teaching can also be found, ranging from full program delivery at an offshore campus, through a combined face-to-face and flexible delivery option, and e-learning (Allport, 2000; Goodfellow, Lea, Gonzalez & Mason, 2001).

Transnational education is constantly evolving. Wilson and Vlăsceanu (2000) distinguished between three inter-related perspectives of this evolution adding that, all these new developments in higher education share certain common characteristics and similarities, mainly in terms of the ways they cross the borders of national higher education systems. It is for this reason that they are usually identified by the generic phrase of transnational education. (Wilson & Vlăsceanu, 2000, p. 75)

The first perspective relates to the delivery mechanisms and arrangements including franchising, corporate universities, international institutions, distance learning, and virtual universities (Machado dos Santos, 2002). Wilson and Vlăsceanu (2000) noted:

One form of development refers to a modality of delivering an educational programme (i.e. distance education), others to ways of establishing a programme/institution (i.e. franchising or twinning/branch campus), and others again to ways of offering primarily continuing education to certain new groups of students. There seems to be no limit to the proliferation of such modalities or arrangements, as long as the demand for higher education is still growing, and the possibilities for a global market continue to emerge. (Wilson & Vlăsceanu, 2000, p. 78)

The second perspective relates to the institutional and organisational arrangements that result from the adopted delivery mechanisms. This can be either: a new institution, a branch, or a franchised program or course of study offering an award within an existing institution or other organisation. The third perspective refers to the nature and quality of qualifications awarded through transnational education for example degrees, certificates, or study credits (Wilson & Vlăsceanu, 2002).

Following on Wilson & Vlăsceanu's (2002) categorisation of transnational programs according to their delivery mechanism, Adam (2001) and Vignoli (2004) have described the most common forms of such programs as follows:

1. **Franchising**: the process whereby a higher education institution (franchiser) from a certain country grants another institution (franchisee) in another country the right to provide the franchiser's programmes/qualifications in the franchisee's host country, irrespective of the students' provenance; in many cases, the franchisee only provides the first part of the educational programme, which can be recognised as partial credits towards a qualification at the franchiser's in the context of a *programme articulation.*

2. **Programme articulations**: inter-institutional arrangements whereby two or more institutions agree to define jointly a study programme in terms of study credits and credit transfer, so that students pursuing their studies in one institution have their credits recognised by the other in order to continue their studies (*twinning programmes, articulation agreements*, etc.). These may -or may not- lead to joint or double degrees.

3. **Branch campus**: a campus established by a higher education institution from one country in another country (host country) to offer its own educational programmes/qualifications, irrespective of the students' provenance; the arrangement is similar to franchising, but the franchisee is a campus of the franchiser.

4. **Off-shore institution**: an autonomous institution established in a host country but said to belong, in terms of its organisation and educational contents, to the education system of some other country, without (necessarily) having a campus in the mother country.

5. **Corporate universities**: they are usually parts of big transnational corporations and organise their own higher education institutions or study programmes offering qualifications that do not belong to any national system of higher education.

6. **International institutions**: institutions offering so-called *international* programmes/qualifications that are not part of a specific education system.

7. **Distance learning arrangements and virtual universities**, where the learner is provided with course material via post or Web-based solutions, and self administers the learning process at home; the only contact with the student is by remote means. (Vignoli, 2004, p. 2)

Bjarnason (2005) further qualified the various types of transnational education programs according to two scales. One scale indicated the extent of on-line reliance of a program and ranged from *wholly face-to-face* to *wholly on-line*; the other indicated the extent of institutional involvement in program development and delivery, ranging from *wholly in-house* to *majority outsource*. Figure 2.4.2.a presents placement of transnational programs according to the two scales.

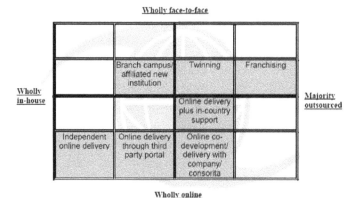

Figure 2.4.2.a. Types of transnational provision.
(As presented in Bjarnason, 2005.)

In Australia, twinning programs represent the typical model of early transnational education. According to McBurnie & Pollock, twinning programs

are similar to the concept of locally supported distance education programs, except that they are fully taught programs following the same syllabus and timetable as the relevant home campus program. Students have the same materials, lectures and examinations as their peers in the provider institution. The academic staff are usually locally engaged, but selected by the provider institution according to its usual criteria. (McBurnie & Pollock, 1998, p. 13)

Davis, Olsen & Böhm (IDP Education Australia, 2000) suggested a typology for Australian transnational education programs in which they separate the provider dimension from the student dimension. The

29

provider dimension of the model spans a range where the increasing responsibility of the partner institution varies across academic teaching, assessment, and support; curriculum; provision of study location; student support; financial administration; and, marketing and promotion. The student dimension includes various modes of delivery from fully face-to-face through supported distance and independent distance to fully online. The two-dimensional model is presented in Figure 2.4.2.b.

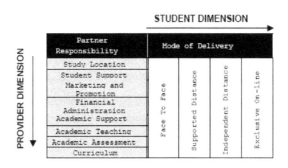

Figure 2.4.2.b. Two-dimensional model of offshore provision.
(As presented in IDP Education Australia, 2000, p. 41.)

According to Davis et al. (IDP Education Australia, 2000), this two-dimensional model offers several advantages. First, it gives the ability to examine transnational programs without having to draw distinction between the student perspective and the provider perspective. Second, it separates the characteristics that describe business models from those that describe teaching and learning models. And finally, it enables the examination of the relationship between the transnational program provider and its partner institution.

2.4.3. Factors determining the demand for and supply of transnational education

The changing nature of demand and supply in transnational tertiary education that has emerged since the late 1990s has been described as the 'business of borderless education' (Cunningham et al, 2000). The demand varies between countries, whereby countries with more rigid education systems tend to attract more transnational providers. Here it often acts as a significant access route to higher education and the acquisition of internationally recognised qualifications (although not necessarily nationally recognised ones). According to Adam (2001), the main determinants of demand include: cost of the program; brand name of the provider and product; value-added from the program; reputation, quality and perceptions of the program; the national/international recognition of the program; the convenience and nature of delivery; and, the level of competition (dissatisfaction/failings of traditional education provision). These determinants can be further separated into *pull factors* that attract students to imported education and *push factors* that repel students from home provision.

According to Marginson (2004b) demand for *cross-border* tertiary education in Asia-Pacific is driven by three factors: (1) insufficient supply of places in local universities, (2) globalisation of work force, and (3) potential status and mobility associated with and acquisition of a foreign degree.

> Demand is driven by three factors. First, in many nations there are insufficient places in reputable degree-granting institutions at home. Second, there are expanding opportunities for globally mobile labour in fields such as business services, ICTs and scientific research. Education in the USA or another English-language nation provides favourable positioning in global labour markets. Third, graduates can use foreign degrees to secure status and mobility benefits. They enhance employment potential at home and abroad, and may open the way to migration to the nation of education or elsewhere. (Marginson, 2004b, p. 85)

Research reveals three main determinants of the supply of transnational education: costs of production of programs (that decrease with increasing scale); the nature of the national market; and, the existence of legal regulation and controls (Marginson, 2002). According to Knight (2004), much of the impetus for transnational education comes directly from the need to raise income by both traditional and *for profit* education providers – the former are increasingly seeking new ways to increase their funding. The supply of transnational education provision is also encouraged by the increasing technical ease of delivery through the use of the Internet and other technologies.

2.4.4. Typical transnational program – operational characteristics

According to the Confederation of European Union Rectors' Conferences (2001) report, transnational education in Europe is largely confined to business subjects (especially MBAs), information technology, computer science and the teaching of widely spoken languages, for example English, Spanish, German. A typical transnational program offered by Australian universities is also in the field of study of business, information technology, and education (IDP Education Australia, 2000; Schoorman, 2000; Welch, 2002). Recent statistics, presented in Table 2.4.4.a, suggest that in the past few years, health has emerged as a popular field of study for transnational students.

Table 2.4.4.a. Overseas students onshore and offshore by field of education,
2001-2003. (AVCC, 2005, p. 4)

	2001	2002	2003
On-Shore Students			
Agriculture, Environment and related studies	835	1,096	1,185
Architecture and Building	2,380	2,861	3,155
Creative Arts	4,497	6,683	7,738
Education	2,181	3,492	4,305
Engineering and Related Technologies	8,263	11,146	13,529
Food, Hospitality and Personal Services	20	19	11
Health	4,809	7,222	8,506
Information Technology	15,440	25,253	25,292
Management and Commerce	30,576	47,296	56,281
Natural and Physical Science	4,210	5,931	6,814
Society and Culture	7,313	9,200	14,121
Non-Award Courses and Mixed Field Programs	3,460	11,440	10,947
Total No. of On-Shore Overseas Students	83,992	131,639	151,884
Off-Shore Students			
Agriculture, Environment and related studies	21	54	50
Architecture and Building	419	659	792
Creative Arts	933	1,217	1,429
Education	625	1,133	1,251
Engineering and Related Technologies	782	2,442	3,265
Food, Hospitality and Personal Services	5	-	-
Health	3,753	4,670	4,322
Information Technology	3,655	5,983	6,631
Management and Commerce	16,251	34,306	37,199
Natural and Physical Science	386	656	791
Society and Culture	1,297	295	2,436
Non-Award Courses	139	2,004	347
Total No. of Off-Shore Overseas Students	28,266	53,419	58,513
Total Overseas Students (No.)	**112,258**	**185,058**	**210,397**

Davis et al. (IDP Education Australia, 2000), having conducted a survey of Australia's offshore programs, provide a list of further characteristics of a typical Australian transnational program. Such a program is offered in Hong Kong, Malaysia or Singapore; these countries host the largest number of Australian transnational programs, as evidenced in Table 2.4.4.b; they also provide the largest number of transnational students, as evidenced in Table 2.4.4.c. Although, the overall offshore student numbers in the top three source countries declined in semester one, 2004 compared to semester two, 2003 (as shown in Table 2.4.4.c), together these markets account for 65% of students in Australian transnational programs; at the same time, there was a strong growth in emerging transnational markets, namely Vietnam, China, and Indonesia (IDP Education Australia, 2004).

Table 2.4.4.b. Current offshore programs of Australian universities
(by year of first intake), pre-2000 – 2003. (AVCC, 2005, p. 11)

	PRE - 2000	2000	2001	2002	2003	Total (a)
Country						
China	98	30	22	24	24	200
Hong Kong (SAR)	154	21	26	23	16	227
Indonesia	15	3	2	1	3	25
Malaysia	174	59	28	24	29	321
Singapore	194	43	30	58	53	375
Other	260	62	39	43	18	421
TOTAL	**895**	**218**	**147**	**173**	**143**	**1569**

Table 2.4.4.c. International students: top 5 markets by detailed
transnational mode. (IDP Education Australia, 2004, p. 12)

Rank	Distance Online	Number	Growth	Offshore on-Campus	Number	Growth
1	Malaysia	3,846	-29%	Singapore	10,986	3%
2	Singapore	2,952	-16%	Hong Kong	9,351	-17%
3	Hong Kong	1,952	-25%	Malaysia	8,126	17%
4	China	1,867	23%	China	5,472	18%
5	Canada	807	-15%	Vietnam	955	47%
	Total	16,053	-15%	Total	41,162	1%

A typical Australian transnational program involves full-time attendance and, in terms of delivery mode, relies on face-to-face teaching or supported distance education; involves a partner which is a private education institution or public education institution; and, awards an Australian qualification (IDP Education Australia, 2000). Recent statistics, presented in Table 2.4.4.c, confirm the prevalence of transnational programs that rely on face-to-face interaction and, with the exception of the Hong Kong market, their increasing growth; the figures also indicate a decline, with the exception of China, in the demand for online programs. Overall, in 2004 the number of distance online students declined by 15% on semester two, 2003, while there was a 1% growth in on-campus students (IDP Education Australian, 2004; refer also to Table 2.2.2.b in Section 2.2.2).

Davies et al. (IDP Education Australia, 2000) provides the following summary of typical transnational programs offered by Australian universities:

- Most of the programs (64%) were offered in Australia's key markets for international students, being Hong Kong, Singapore, and Malaysia,
- Highest enrolments in offshore programs were in Hong Kong, Malaysia, China, and Singapore,
- More than 25% of programs had commenced in the last year, thus indicating substantial expansion of Australia's offshore education provision,
- The awards for the programs were provided by the Australian university,
- Most of the partner organizations (55%) were private and public education institutions,
- Delivery of almost 80% of programs was classified as being face-to-face or supported distance. (IDP Education Australia, 2000, p. 45)

In terms of responsibility, the Australian university is responsible for curriculum, teaching assessment, and quality assurance, and allocates to the offshore partner responsibility for provision of study location, marketing, promotion and financial administration. Although, on the whole, the Australian university is responsible for the quality assurance of the program, partner institutions, overseas governments, and international organisations also participate in this responsibility (IDP Education Australia, 2000).

2.4.5. The importance of the face-to-face component

Although many universities view online learning as an economic alternative to face-to-face teaching (Davis & Meares, 2001), online learning cannot be regarded as a suitable alternative in transnational settings (Emil, 2001). This view is also supported by Tomasic who claims that:

> Electronic delivery of courses to off-shore destinations is unlikely to be seen as an acceptable substitute for face
> to face delivery, although greater use of electronic means to deliver parts of courses may be acceptable
> (Tomasic, 2002, p. 11).

Fully online provision of transnational programs raises many concerns regarding the learning experience, particularly about the extent of feedback and guidance that can be provided to students (Herrmann, Downie, & O'Connell, 2001; Knipe, 2002). Debowski (2003) agrees that fully online provision of offshore programs is generally perceived to be less effective than options including a face-to-face component. She emphasises the strong recognition of the value of (Australian) academics meeting and interacting with the offshore students population; such regular teaching input by these academics significantly enriches the transnational program (Debowski, 2003).

Another aspect of transnational education that benefits from face-to-face interactions is localisation of teaching. As Ziguras (2000) pointed out, the curriculum of a transnational program is usually standardised across several campuses, which may be located in different countries. While the curriculum is sometimes tailored to local conditions, the modifications are usually minimal; they may only involve assignment questions for example. In such circumstances, teachers, through face-to-face interaction, can play an important role contextualising and interpreting the content of study materials to make it useful for their students.

> Face-to-face teachers are able to introduce a significant degree of local interpretation for imported educational
> materials. Being in close contact with students, they are in a position to know how much local contextualisation
> these materials may require, and can achieve a balance in the use of various types of material according to
> students' level, interests, language skills, and so on. (Ziguras, 2000, p. 33)

> The relationship between students and face-to-face teachers is crucial in making foreign materials relevant to
> students. (Ziguras, 2000, p. 33)

The importance of the face-to-face communication and the need for localisation of transnational programs was also raised by Evans & Tregenza (2002). They examined a range of transnational programs offered in Hong Kong by Australian universities in collaboration with Hong Kong partner institutions. They commented on provision of face-to-face tuition in those programs concluding that *Hong Kong students seek and expect such contact*. They also pointed out that both the Australian instructors as well as Hong Kong tutors agreed *that the Australian courses need to be adapted to suit the needs of Hong Kong*

34

students; to this end, Australian instructors would localise study materials, and face-to-face Hong Kong tutors would put those materials in relevant context. However, the extent of course localisation was limited by the existing regulatory framework (Evans & Tregenza, 2002). It should be noted that under Hong Kong legislation, all award granting programs offered by transnational (non-local) institutions must be registered; the registration criteria include the following condition:

> In the case of a course leading to the award of non-local higher academic qualification, the course must be offered by a recognised institution and is itself recognized by its home country as being of a comparable standard to a similar course operated by the institution in the home country. (Hong Kong Government, 1996, Section 10, p. A666)

Although some advanced technologies, such as streaming media technologies are very capable of supporting voice and video and afford the possibility to emulate face-to-face interaction, they may be out of reach for many distance learners. For example, videoconferencing for learning over the Internet requires more bandwidth that is usually available to a regular Internet subscriber (Hentea, Shea & Pennington, 2003).

The availability of technology is not the only prohibitive factor; there are also aspects of curriculum and teaching that are difficult to emulate through technology. For instance, *demonstration of theoretical knowledge in Internet classes is below that of traditional classes* (Marold & Haga, 2004, p. 16). Having measured online students' ability to apply programming theory, Marold & Haga concluded that the Internet did not lend itself to the deployment of subjects that involved problem solving and higher analytical reasoning, such as advanced computing subjects – the online students in their study performed significantly worse than their counterparts in a traditional classroom. Discussing the results, the authors identified several factors that determined poorer performance of online learners in their study including: inadequate instructional methods, technology differences, and differences in group interaction. With respect to instructional methods, they pointed out that

> instruction in the online environment is still in its infancy and faculty, as instructors and course designers, have not yet developed the most effective methods for delivering some type of content in this context. (Marold & Haga, 2004, p. 17)

On the subject of technology, Marold & Haga highlighted the fact that face-to-face interaction created opportunities that let

> Classroom instructors emphasize important content and encourage application of that content in ways that are not even apparent to the instructor – often through subtle changes in voice or body language that are simply instinctive for effective instructors. (Marold & Haga, 2004, p. 17)

They went on to say that application of theory in particular, might be effectively illustrated in the classroom through the choice of suitable examples or through answers to students' questions; technology could not easily emulate this kind of interaction. Moreover, *simple repetition can be effective in a classroom, but it is difficult to implement online* (Marold & Haga, 2004, p. 17). The authors also

35

suggested that group interaction in a classroom setting could be an important contributor to the learning process. However, this kind of interaction is difficult to emulate in the online environment even through thoughtful use of online forums, chat sessions, and email; *the cohesiveness and satisfaction of class discovery is not duplicated online* (Marold & Haga, 2004, p. 17).

Related to the importance of direct group interaction is the community aspect of face-to-face contact (Chen, 1997). Chen found that dialogue not only allows students to assess their learning, but also to develop a sense of community with other students; this sense of community can alleviate the problem of isolation often reported by distance students. Kirkup & Jones (1996) agree and state that *students need dialogue with their teachers and with other students in order to consolidate and check on their own learning* (p. 278). Moreover, they list the inability to offer dialogue in the way that conventional face-to-face education does as one of three most significant weaknesses of distance education; the inflexibility of content and study method, and the isolation and individualisation of the student are cited as the remaining two weaknesses.

It should also be noted that even universal access to computers by offshore students is not a safe assumption. For example, Singh and Han (2004) while working at Jilin University in China, found that many of their academic colleagues and students had limited access to a personal desktop computer, the Internet, and email; they had to pay for timed access to their email accounts and for downloading attachments; and, they did not have access to high-speed data networks. For those users, their offline education could be supplemented, but not replaced, by ever-advancing online technologies (Singh & Han, 2004).

In China the limited equipment and infrastructure for transnational online education in many institutions is only one factor that reduces its viability; one other important factor is *the strict legislation of central government regarding online education services provided by foreign countries* (Huang, 2003, p. 203).

In addition, students who have to rely solely on online learning may have reduced opportunity to develop a broad range of learning skills, which may be possible under the guidance of a teacher *in situ*. However, this problem may be alleviated if teachers involved in the delivery of an online program are well trained in conveying such skills through good program design (Oliver, 2000).

Research studies have indicated the importance of face-to-face interaction (Marold & Haga, 2003), and demonstrated that quality in education can be achieved by incorporating computer technology and face-to-face interaction (Kiser, 2002). Marold's study of performance and achievement between online students and classroom students found that achievement tended to be higher in the Web students.

However, performance on projects and homework submissions was found to be higher in classroom students; especially in programming classes, online students with an average ability level had more difficulty applying the theory of programming problems than classroom students (Marold, Larsen, & Moreno, 2000).

Kiser (2002) reported on a two-year study by Thomson Learning. Launched in 1999, the study compared the results of three sets of adult learners: the first – the *blended* group – were taught to use Microsoft Excel with a mix of online and face-to-face instruction; the second group took an online course; the third group – the control group – received no training. The study report concluded that the blended group performed tasks 30% more accurately than the online-only group. The blended group and online group both performed better than the control group with no training in accuracy, by 159% and 99% respectively. In addition, the blended group performed tasks 41% faster than the online group.

A recent meta-study aimed at identifying factors that affect the effectiveness of distance education has led to some important data-driven conclusions including the importance of face-to-face communication, live human instructors, and the right mixture of human involvement and technology (Zhao, Lei, Yan, Lai & Tan, 2005). Zhao et al. suggested that programs combining face-to-face component and technology mediated distance component resulted in the most positive outcomes.

Given the importance of face-to-face interaction, successful distance education programs are increasingly moving towards a new model known as *blended* or *hybrid* distance learning. The hybrid model adds a human touch to distance learning by using facilitators or mentors and promoting various types of interactions between students, instructors, and resource centers (Hentea et al., 2003; Riffee, 2003; Zhao et al., 2005). Some of the successful distance education programs which blend the traditional distance learning model with face-to-face teaching sessions include the programs at Purdue University West Lafayette, Indiana University, and Penn State University (Hentea et al., 2003). Riffee (2003) supports the hybrid approach maintaining that media alone cannot offer students guidance and personal engagement. Consequently, he regards face-to-face interaction as a necessary ingredient of successful distance education:

> I am fortunate to be associated with distance education programs that are very successful from the point of view of learning outcomes and that have been academically successful. It is my opinion that much of that success comes from using a hybrid model of distance education that involves the electronic delivery of content coupled with face-to-face contact by a faculty facilitator or mentor. (Riffee, 2003, p. 10)

Ziguras (2002) pointed out the importance of face-to-face interaction in transnational programs and decreasing interest in such programs if provided fully online; recent statistics, presented in Table 2.4.4.c in Section 2.4.4, confirm the declining interest in online programs. Having examined various modes of transnational program delivery in Australia and elsewhere, Ziguras suggested that the future of transnational programs belongs to programs that include face-to-face interaction facilitated largely by an offshore partner of the educational provider; he uses the term *joint delivery* to describe such programs.

> Evidence internationally shows that fully on-line delivery is proving unpopular except in small niche programmes, due to the lack of face-to-face contact, an unwillingness on the part of students to pay high fees and significant start-up costs. Branch campuses are faced with problems of scale and expose the provider to considerable financial risk through capital investment offshore. Perhaps the best approach, both in terms of mode of delivery and financial risk, is seen to be "joint delivery" with local, established partners, using on-line delivery in some form (for enrolment and general information for example). This approach still requires an on-going commitment to building quality partnerships, and rigorous internal approvals. (Ziguras, 2002)

In brief, this section discussed various aspects of one particular model of distance education, which is the subject of this research study, namely transnational education. The section reviewed the definition of transnational education, its typology, growth, factors influencing the demand for and supply of transnational education, characteristics of typical programs, as well as the role of face-to-face interaction in those programs.

2.5. SPECIAL REQUIREMENTS OF COMPUTING EDUCATION AT A DISTANCE

The previous section (Section 2.4) focused on the transnational type of distance education. The section presented an overview of transnational education including its typology and operational characteristics. This section continues on by outlining the particular demands of computing education offered at a distance.

In addition to the standard problems of distance education the aspects of each individual field of study introduce unique problems. In the field of computing, two aspects present a unique challenge: the ever-changing nature of computing, and the need for students to have access to appropriate computing resources.

Change is one of the defining characteristics of computing. As a consequence, the production and design of up-to-date distance education material results in high costs (Murgatroyd & Woudstra, 1990). Investing considerable resources in developing subject material that must change every time it is offered may not be economically viable. This is especially true in advanced computing subjects where there is a small student population (Jones, 1996).

The study of computing includes three essential paradigms: theory, abstraction and design (Denning et al., 1989). In addition, the study of computing necessitates substantial hands-on practical experience. To learn the abstraction and design paradigms and to gain practical computing experience, students must have access to appropriate computing resources, and this need presents one of the biggest challenges to offering distance education programs in computing.

The study of computing, particularly at an advanced level, involves problem solving skills, critical thinking skills, and application of theory. Research has found that computing subjects requiring and aiming to develop these advanced skills were not sufficiently effective when offered at a distance (Marold & Haga, 2004; Terry, 2001). Marold & Haga (2004) conducted a study comparing three offerings – two online and one classroom – of a programming subject in Visual Basic. The results of this study showed a significant difference in the means of student projects and tests that required application of theory learned – online students scored significantly lower; they also performed significantly worse in theory portions of exams and in projects. The results indicated that online distance *students are having trouble applying concepts of programming that they are attempting to learn* (Marold & Haga, 2004, p. 16). The authors concluded that, while more research was needed, the design and delivery of online problem solving subjects needed careful attention.

Students in traditional computing programs have access to on-campus computer laboratories; however, this is not a universally appropriate solution for distance education students. Holmberg & Bakshi (1982), and Kember (1982) discuss the issue and offer models for institutions to follow in meeting this 'practical' requirement, for instance residential schools, or local centers. Xenos et al. (2002) report that more recently the standard approach has been to require distance computing students to secure their own computing access. This generally results in computing students facing greater expense in order to purchase appropriate hardware, software, training and support (Xenos et al., 2002).

The growing availability of personal computers at home means that most students are able to gain access to a computer. However, problems may occur with some advanced subjects that require capabilities and performance not available on personal computers. For instance, some systems may need to contain both the domain knowledge and behaviour embedded through programming, others may require access to high speed Internet connections; those types of requirements cannot be easily met by individual distance learners (Hentea et al., 2003). At some institutions, residential schools provide access to these resources; other institutions do not use residential schools. Some institutions address this problem by supporting several computer platforms available to students; others specify a standard computing platform and design all subjects for that platform. Designing a subject for multiple platforms introduces additional problems and requires a considerably higher investment of resources than designing for a single platform.

Achieving consensus from a group of academics on a single suitable computing platform may also be difficult (Jones, 1996).

The availability of software presents another difficulty. With on-campus computing laboratories it is possible to organise site licences for required software. Obtaining similar site licences that allow the supply of software to distance students is rare. This results in distance students having to purchase the necessary software, thus further adding to the costs of the distance program.

Lastly, there is the issue of support. According to Jones (1996), distance computing students demonstrate varying levels of computing expertise. While some students will have years of experience in the computing industry, others will be familiar with only basic computer functions. Novice computing users about to study computing by distance education will face two challenges: first, they must become familiar with the operation of distance education and how best to fit study into their existing life style; and, second, they must obtain, install, configure, and learn how to use a computer. These novice students require additional assistance from the lecturers of first year subjects and technical support staff (Jones, 1996). However, a more recent study by Xenos, Pierrakeas, & Pintelas (2002) does not share Jones's concerns regarding novice students, concluding that the majority of students who choose to study computing by distance are already familiar with this field, and either own a computer or use a computer and e-mail.

To summarise, this section highlighted the unique demands of computing by distance education: firstly, the requirement to update study material in a rapidly changing discipline; secondly, the need to teach subjects involving theory, higher analytical reasoning, and problem solving; and finally, the requirement to accommodate hardware and software needs of the students.

2.6. EFFECTIVENESS OF DISTANCE EDUCATION/TRANSNATIONAL EDUCATION PROGRAMS

Following on the discussion of transnational education presented in Section 2.4, and the overview of the particular demands of computing education offered in transnational mode discussed in Section 2.5, this section focuses on the issue of effectiveness of transnational education programs. The section reviews the definition of effectiveness in transnational context, as well as determinants, and measures of program effectiveness.

2.6.1. Effectiveness of transnational programs – definition and perspectives

A distance education program is perceived to be effective if it fulfills the needs of its participants to such an extent that they would be happy to enrol in another similarly designed program (Merisotis & Phipps, 1999). The needs of the learners represent individually and socially defined goals that can be achieved in a variety of ways and relate to a number of learning outcomes. Although the ultimate objective of a program is to enable the learners to achieve their goals, the assessment of its effectiveness invariably involves evaluation of factors at two levels of operation: the individual level and the system level. At the individual level, the learning experience, the practical relevance of acquired skills, and satisfaction with the learning experience are evaluated. At the system level, the evaluation includes the functional, managerial and instructional aspects (Chute et al., 1999).

Students perceive a distance education program to be effective if they pass examinations, feel that the content of the program is relevant to their needs, have an opportunity to network with other students, feel part of the class and connected to teachers, have opportunities for participation, receive support when needed, experience few technical problems, and feel comfortable with the technology (Neal, 1999; Simonson et al., 2000; Stein, 1998).

Teachers perceive a program to be effective if students are motivated, complete assessment tasks and participate in discussion, use the technology to communicate, pass examinations and few students drop out from the program. Teachers also perceive the program to be effective if the program content meets the students' needs, and if the institution provides financial, personnel and technical support.

From the perspective of distance education program developers, effective programs are designed to meet diverse needs of students (Keast, 1997; Knott, 1992; Thompson, 1998). Students in distance education programs represent a wide variety of backgrounds, experiences and needs which make it impossible to identify the *typical* distance student (Charp, 1997). Therefore, an effective distance education program has to cater for varied student profiles. The effectiveness of a program can be further enhanced if developers understand and apply learning theories to its development and delivery (Pallof & Pratt, 1999; Trilling & Hood, 1999).

From an educational perspective, an effective distance education program should support the universal principles for good practice in education. It should encourage and maximise contacts between students and teachers, develop relationships and promote collaboration among students, incorporate active learning, give rich and rapid feedback to students, stress time-on-task, set high standards for students' performance, and respect individual differences and allow students opportunities for learning that acknowledge those differences (Chickering & Ehrmann, 1996; Chickering & Gamson, 1987; McLoughlin, Oliver & Wood 1999).

2.6.2. Determinants of program effectiveness

The growth of distance education has necessitated responses regarding two issues: pedagogical changes facilitated and imposed by advances in distance education technologies; and, the effectiveness of distance education (Nasseh, 1997). According to Nasseh (1997), questions concerning effectiveness of distance education relate to learner characteristics and needs, course effectiveness, course outcomes, instructional design, and comparisons with traditional mode of study.

Phipps & Merisotis (2000), following a review of program quality measures used by leading distance education institutions, identified seven categories considered essential to ensuring excellence in distance education, especially Internet-based. The categories include: institutional support, course development, teaching/learning, course structure, student support, staff support, and evaluation and assessment.

The amount of interaction in a program appears to be an important element of its effectiveness. Interaction can be defined as *an interplay and exchange in which individuals and groups influence each other* (Rovai & Barnum, 2003, p. 59). Moore (1990) points to the content of the interaction between teacher and student and the quality of the communication system facilitating this interaction as determinants of successful distance education. Morgan & McKenzie (2003) and Palloff & Pratt (1999) also stress the critical importance of interaction between participants in the distance education environment and regard it as one of the determinants of effectiveness. Carefully designed and well conducted, interaction has the potential to turn a distance education program, particularly a Web-based one, to an educational experience:

> A well-delivered course provides multiple means by which students and the instructor can interact, including e-mail, discussion boards, and careful use of synchronous discussion. The effective use of the means by which interactivity is enhanced deepens the learning experience and creates a more satisfying outcome for everyone. Content can be creatively delivered through facilitation of effective, Internet research, and companion Websites both on and outside of the course site. When content is delivered in multiple ways, it also addresses different student learning styles and creates an interesting course overall. But it is the interaction and connections made in the course that students will remember as the keys to learning in an online course. (Palloff & Pratt, 2001, p. 153)

According to Gallagher & McCormick (1999), research on distance education effectiveness has focused on four domains:

(1) student attitude and satisfaction regarding delivery of coursework;

(2) interactions of students and instructors during delivery of coursework;

42

(3) student outcomes in distance education coursework; and

(4) instructor satisfaction with delivery and coursework

In addition, Spooner et al. (1999) have analysed many studies based on comparative features such as cognitive factors including the amount of learning, academic performance, achievement, and examination and assignment grades; and other factors, including student satisfaction, comfort, convenience, and communication with instructor, interaction and collaboration between students, independence, and perceptions of effectiveness. Recent studies have focused on specific characteristics in distance education including student satisfaction (Allen, Bourhis, Burrell, & Mabry, 2002); instructional features affecting student achievement (Machtmes & Asher, 2000); and education technologies in learning (Cavanaugh, 2001).

Since distance education is a fusion of education and technology to deliver instructions effectively to students at a distance, the key to an effective distance education program is the effectiveness of the individual components and the flexibility of the interface between them. Some educators argue that the lack of interaction, student-to-student and student-to-teacher, is one of the biggest challenges. Studies show however, that when distance education techniques are used properly, non-traditional interaction can be as effective as the conventional face-to-face interaction (Bernt & Bugbee, 1993; Howell & Jayaratna, 2000).

2.6.3. Measures of program effectiveness

A major concern about distance education continues to be its quality compared to traditional classroom education – *Although students may like the flexibility offered by distance learning, there continues to be concern about the quality of those programs* (Sonner, 1999, p. 243). This concern has spurred extensive research into the factors that could measure the quality of these programs. In many cases, 'broad' measures of the effectiveness of distance education have been examined such as: academic performance, satisfaction, attitudes, and evaluation of instruction.

Effectiveness of distance education programs is often measured by the programs' outcomes. Research into the learning outcomes of students in distance education has found that they are very similar to those within the traditional classroom (Fox, 1998; Sonner, 1999). Although student achievement is one common measure of a distance education program's success, it is not the most descriptive one. Additional models of distance education effectiveness that have been suggested include the Flashlight Project, and studies on learner traits and media variables that is, Aptitude-Treatment Interaction (ATI) studies (Holmberg, 1995; Keegan, 1996; Thorpe, 1988, as cited in Lockee, Burton, & Cross, 1999).

The Flashlight Project helps educators study and evaluate educational uses of technology. It was initiated in 1992 by the Teaching, Learning and Technology affiliate of the American Association for Higher Education. The project involved the development of a suite of evaluation tools, including validated survey items, interview questions, and cost analysis methods, that educational institutions could use to study and steer their own uses of technology. One of the tools enables monitoring the usefulness of technology in distance education programs and its impact on learning outcomes; for example, the student's ability to apply what was learned in the academic program. Another tool helps investigators design models of how programs use money, space and time. All of these efforts are directed toward gathering information about the interaction of staff and students in the digital classroom (Ehrmann, 2005). The Flashlight Project is cited as an outstanding example of a model for effective distance education evaluation (Lockee et al., 1999).

The Aptitude-Treatment Interaction research approach is based on the assumption that instructional environment and learning characteristics can interact in ways that affect learning outcomes. It relies on the concept that some instructional strategies are more or less effective for particular individuals depending upon their specific abilities. As a theoretical framework, ATI suggests that optimal learning results when the instruction is exactly matched to the aptitudes of the learner. The assumption is that those with less of a specific ability are qualitatively and quantitatively different and not just slower, and this difference may be dealt with if different methods are used to support learning. The aim of this approach is to develop instructions that do not fit the average person but fit groups of students with particular aptitude patterns. This way, adaptive learning environments and instruction can be created that identify and address aggregate types or segmented populations of learners, resulting in *mass customisation* (Sigala, 2004).

One other model of evaluation of distance education effectiveness involves assessment of cognitive and motivational characteristics of learners enrolled in Web-based instruction (Lockee et al., 1999). Recent meta-analysis studies have focused on specific characteristics in distance education: student satisfaction (Allen et al., 2002); instructional features affecting learner achievement (Machtmes & Asher, 2000); and education technologies (Cavanaugh, 2001).

In brief, this section introduced the issue of effectiveness of transnational education programs. It discussed the definition of program effectiveness and its determinants; it also outlined methods by which to measure program effectiveness.

2.7. FACTORS CONTRIBUTING TO PROGRAM EFFECTIVENESS

Following on the overview of effectiveness of transnational education programs presented in Section 2.6, this section examines the particular factors that contribute to program effectiveness including: the attributes of students and staff involved in the programs; program design and evaluation; technology; and, organisational support.

While the research into distance education has focused largely on student achievement and student satisfaction, the outcomes can determine only 'if' a program was successful, but do not determine 'why' it was successful. According to the literature, it is more important to know why a program was successful than that it met its objectives (Dhanarajan, 1999). Merisotis & Phipps (1999) support this view adding that little attention has been given to the various aspects determining the distance education context. This section attempts to fill that void by examining the various aspects of the distance education milieu with a focus on effectiveness.

2.7.1. Attributes of students

Although it is difficult to summarise the characteristics of all distance learners, literature points out to self-discipline, motivation, and ability to balance multiple roles as determinants of success. In addition, since most distance education programs are student-centered, students have to be able to assume responsibility for the learning process if they are to successfully complete such programs (Saba, 2000). Granger & Benke (1998) characterise a successful distance learner as goal-oriented. Chyung, Winiecki & Fenner (1998) identify the ability of distance learners to adapt to a new mode of learning as one of the characteristics determining success.

Since the majority of distance education students are adults in full time employment, their educational aspirations must usually compete with work, family, and social lives. Therefore, to succeed, they have to balance their studies with family and career demands (Garland, 1993; Granger & Benke, 1998; Morgan & Tam, 1999). Employment in a field where career advances can be readily *achieved through academic upgrading in a distance education environment* also contributes to successful learning (Ross & Powell, 1990, p. 10). Bajtelsmit (1998) emphasised the influence of the external environment, especially the student's family and job, as well as distance learning skills as factors influencing distant student's success and retention (Ross & Powell, 1990). In addition to balancing education, career and family responsibilities, Saba (2000) asserted that time management skills are a contributing factor in the success of the distance student.

45

Kember (1995) developed a two-track model of student persistence in distance education programs, which includes variables grouped under the following headings: student entry characteristics; social integration; external attribution; academic integration, and academic incompatibility (Kember, 1995, p. 64). Kember maintains that the students' previous experiences direct them toward one of two possible pathways in a distance education program. Those with a favourable background in terms of expectations, motivation, and previous experiences, tend to follow the positive track integrating well socially and academically with the institution, program, and instructor. On the other hand, students lacking the favourable background take a negative track where they have difficulties achieving social and academic integration, which affects their achievement in the program. Hence, students on the positive track have a much higher chance of satisfactory achievement in the program.

Cornell & Martin (1997) listed three factors as predictors of student success in distance education: intention to complete the course, early submission of work, and completion of other distance education courses. Billings (1988) also found that students who made the most progress were those who had the intention of completing the program in a specific period of time, submitted their assessment tasks relatively early, had a supportive family, had high goals for completing the program, and had good prerequisite knowledge. However, he singled out the student's intention to complete as the most important factor, which suggests the importance of motivation over other factors. Visser (1998), and Kember (1999) agreed, claiming that motivation is recognised as a facet of students' approach to learning and is the key not only to student progress but also retention in the program.

Another aspect that affects students' success in distance education programs is their attitude towards the technology involved (Christensen, Anakwe & Kessler, 2001; Irons, Jung & Keel, 2002; Valentine, 2002). The research shows that comfort with technology being used in a distance education program is a major factor in determining student satisfaction and success. Fahy & Archer (1999) have found students' prior experience with technology, confidence in the use of technology, and belief that technology would *work effectively for them* to be major predictors of whether a student would choose to participate and succeed in distance learning. Fahy & Archer further suggested that it was not only a matter of having access to, and being familiar with, computers but rather the students' real or perceived lack of skills, *confidence or experience necessary to become truly comfortable with technology as an instrument for learning* (Fahy & Archer, 1999, p. 18). Lim (2001) also found that students' confidence in their ability to use technology and learn new computing skills were linked with the students' positive expectations of success, which then improved performance.

While some student competencies are specific to the technologies used in the program, other competencies, also associated with successfully completing a distance education program, are not related to technology; these include: self-confidence, a commitment to success, preparedness and self-direction (Burge, 1994, p. 34); being focused, having good time management skills and the ability to work independently and as group members, as well as *strong self-motivation, self-discipline, and assertiveness* (Hardy & Boaz, 1997, p. 42); being risk-taking, creative problem solvers (Brown, 1998); having the confidence to follow directions and to ask for assistance when necessary, tolerance for delays in receiving a response from the instructor, time to work on the course, and good comprehension skills (Bernt & Bugbee, 1993).

2.7.2. Attributes of staff involved in the programs

The roles of the instructors, designers, managers and support staff involved in distance education program are crucial. While their roles are just as important in traditional education, distance education presents additional challenges brought upon by the shift of place and time. The literature identifies numerous attributes of distance education staff as critical to the effectiveness of distance education programs. Although these attributes can be separated into three categories of instructor, designer, and manager, many of these attributes overlap across categories.

2.7.2.1. Attributes of instructor

Distance students require a significant amount of information prior to and at the beginning of a program. The focus of distance student recruitment, while ensuring students meet admission and program requirements, also includes ensuring students understand and are equipped to meet the requirements of the program delivery. This focus on recruitment includes advertising both the program and the student competencies necessary to complete the program (Fahy & Archer, 1999).

Research suggests that the effectiveness of distance learning is based on the instructor's preparation, appreciation of the needs of the students, and understanding of the target population (Omoregie, 1997). Meeting the needs of distance learners requires organised, thoughtful strategies to ensure learners have the skills they need to successfully complete a distance education course.

The first step in identifying distance education student needs is to know who the students are, *what's available to them,...their needs and limitations...* in relation to the program (Granger & Benke, 1998, pp. 127-128). Parker (1997) suggests that students entering a distance education context require a change in skills from *simple information processing to autonomous self-motivated learning* and a change in their ability to *interact with the technology* (Parker, 1997, p. 7). The skills of a self-directed learner may or may not be already developed by the student, and need to be addressed directly, with specific instructional strategies. Technological competencies of the students can be assessed during the recruitment process. Information about the students' interests in online instruction, prior experience with the Internet, and technical skills can be obtained upon enrolment to help instructors identify possible student needs for support.

Instructors must have technological skills and confidence to use all of the various electronic media to be effective in a distance education program. Instructors must also change the manner in which they deliver information. When the traditional lecture mode does not work well, other modes of delivery such as multimedia presentations might be more successful (Weber, 1996). Wolcott (1996) (cited in Carter, 2001) found in a study of adult distance learning that

> to effectively bridge the gaps between classroom and distance teaching, faculty need to look at the distance teaching from the students' point of view (Carter, 2001, p. 249).

According to the literature, instructors who teach in distance education programs are perceived as effective if they encourage three types of communication and interaction: firstly, communication and interaction between instructors and students; secondly, among students; and, thirdly, through instructional materials (Moore & Kearsley, 2005). Effective instructors listen and respond to students' needs; they seek feedback from students and incorporate this feedback in the design and delivery of instruction. These instructors enable collaborative learning; they are regarded not merely as presenters of knowledge but rather as its suppliers, and they encourage students to regard each other as information resources. Other attributes of effective distance education instructors include: clear communication of program objectives and requirements to students; use of technology as a tool and not a replacement for teaching; and, willingness to listen to students' suggestions. These instructors are student-centered, sensitive to their anxieties, and are willing to participate in students' experiences (Carr, 2000; Moore & Kearsley, 2005; Roblyer & Wiencke, 2003). Stark & Warne (1999) concur that distance learners expect distance teachers to be interested in the learners as individuals and provide reassurance, support, advice and motivation.

Instructor experience with distance education and good teaching skills are important factors to the effectiveness of a program (Carr, 2000). Carr investigated student satisfaction with the instructors' teaching ability and concluded that many instructors in distance education programs lack teaching experience. As a consequence, students faced with poor quality teaching can become discouraged and frustrated with the programs. Carr reported that students cited inexperienced teachers as one of the reasons for withdrawing from distance education programs. According to Wilkes & Burnham (1991), students who report dissatisfaction with the distance education program because of poor quality teaching are negatively impacted. Students expect the instructor to provide support and guidance, and when they experience unsatisfactory teaching, their success may be put at risk.

Palloff & Pratt (1999) identified the characteristics of effective distance education instructors through the roles of an online instructor. They identified four types of roles: pedagogical, social, managerial, and technical. It is important to note that these roles are applicable to many types of distance education and not only to online education. The pedagogical role sees the instructor as a facilitator of the program providing guidance and motivation to students. Therefore, it is essential that the instructor should provide constructive feedback on assignments and projects, and respond to student emails and postings online. The social role of the instructor serves to promote socialisation in the program (mainly communication within the program) including: communication between instructors and students, communication between students, chat room discussions, and collaborative group projects. Students in distance education programs often feel isolated and instructor's attention to the student's social needs becomes vital. The managerial role of a distance education instructor is one of a decision maker and enforcer and includes establishing program objectives, policies, syllabi, and deadlines (Palloff & Pratt, 1999). Additional responsibilities involve timely marking of assignments and examinations, as well as determining final results for program units. The technical role requires the instructor to be familiar with the technology used in the delivery of the program. Familiarity with the technology is required so that the instructor can assist students experiencing technical difficulties with the multimedia used in the delivery of the program.

It is important for the instructors to develop a sense of community, achieve maximum participation, and engage students in the process (Hiltz & Wellman, 1997). The idea of learning as a collaborative process is very important to distance education students. According to Palloff and Pratt,

> collaborative learning processes assists students to achieve deeper levels of knowledge generation through the creation of shared goals, shared exploration, and a shared process of meaning making. (Palloff & Pratt, 2000, p. 6)

It is up to the instructor to be aware of this in the distance learning environment and to encourage collaborative learning and a sense of community among the students.

2.7.2.2. Attributes of designer

Distance educators also participate in the design of distance education programs. Effective designers have the ability to create tasks and activities that promote interaction and socialisation among students and, while planning those tasks and activities, take into consideration the profiles and learning styles of the students. According to literature, effective designers use reflective enquiry on their own teaching and, during the design process, keep two questions in mind: firstly, whether a particular approach will work; and, secondly, how it could be improved, taking into consideration the learning task, teaching material and strategies, as well as technology involved. These designers regard technology as a tool to create and support learning communities for students; and, when designing learning materials, they also take into consideration past experiences of students (Buchanan, 2000; Palloff & Pratt, 2000; Ragan, 1999; Willis, 1995.)

Since new technologies have enabled new ways of communication and teaching, distance educators need to adjust their roles accordingly. Consequently, the role of the distance educator is changing from a 'sage on stage' to an enabler and guide. The literature points out that, as a result of this change, it is important for distance educators to keep upgrading their skills in three areas: developing interaction, developing instructional materials, and applying technologies (Schauer, Rockwell, Fritz, & Marx, 1998). At the same time, support for staff development is increasingly regarded as an integral part of the changing distance education environment (Granger & Benke, 1998). The growth of this environment has necessitated educators not only with competence in their subject area, but also with interest and skills in technology; educators with such skills can take advantage of additional technology-enabled teaching methods and thereby provide effective distance education experiences for students (Schweb, Kelley, & Orr 1998).

2.7.2.3. Attributes of manager

In addition to their roles as instructors and designers, distance educators play the role of managers. According to the literature, attributes of effective distance educators as managers include timely distribution of learning materials and timely feedback to students on assignments and projects. Effective managers also ensure that the required classroom equipment is available and operational, and are prepared for potential problems with technology. In addition, they are knowledgeable about the academic resources available to students (Palloff & Pratt, 1999).

2.7.3. Program design

A number of research studies have examined the relationship between student perceptions and program characteristics. St.Pierre & Olson (1991) (as cited in Moore & Kearsley, 2005) identified several factors as contributors to student satisfaction and success in distance education programs including: a good study guide, relevant course content, the opportunity to apply knowledge, prompt return of assignments, and conversations with instructors. In addition, Egan, Sebastian & Welch (1991) established that distant learners benefit significantly from a well-designed syllabus and presentation outlines. On the other hand, Hara & Kling (1999) reported on factors having the most negative impact on student progression and satisfaction including: unclear instructions for assignments, lack of timely feedback on assignments and projects, and technical problems. Thus the characteristics associated with program design essentially revolve around two factors – instruction and interaction.

2.7.3.1. Instruction

The literature identifies quality of instruction as a factor that affects student success in distance education programs (Frew & Webber, 1995; Inman & Kerwin, 1999). Quality of instruction includes the timely provision of teaching materials, quality of the program, quality of teaching, and the performance of the instructors.

The quality of instruction influences the quality of student learning. Learning tasks can be designed using a range of methods to achieve valid learning objectives; the assessment system associated with those tasks influences the extent to which students will pursue those desirable learning outcomes. Therefore, it is critical to ensure that assessment tasks are integrated with learning objectives (Freeman & Capper, 1999).

With respect to transnational programs, there is an increasing expectation that offshore teaching will encompass both face-to-face and electronic guidance through the curriculum; this kind of support helps students gain a stable, richer, and more encompassing learning experience. As a consequence of this expectation, teachers involved in transnational programs need to become proficient in the area of e-learning to be able to develop electronic resources and support, online tutorials and other forms of technology-supported guidance (Debowski, 2003).

Graphic design is considered an important and powerful tool for instructional design in distance learning (Ouyang & Fu, 1996). However, not all graphics automatically enhance distance learning. According to Rieber (as cited in Ouyang & Fu, 1996), the effectiveness of instructional graphics largely depends on the nature of the learning task and the profile of the learner; to be effective, graphics should be matched with the instructional objectives. Rieber identified five instructional applications of graphics: cosmetic, motivation, attention-gaining, presentation, and practice. While the first two instructional applications aim to enhance the affective appeal of a lesson, the latter three endeavour to directly enhance the cognitive abilities of students to learn from study materials. Consequently, the primary purpose for designing graphics should be to aid, enhance, or support distance education.

Relevance of subject matter and the way in which it is communicated are critical to the success of distance education programs. Simon (1994) claims that *human beings are at their best when they interact with the real world and draw lessons from the bumps and bruises they hit* (p. 74). Capper (1999) also notes that research-based evidence emphasises more explicit links between theory and real-life application. She also stresses the importance of providing students with a detailed and realistic description of what they can expect from the distance learning program. This is particularly important to adult learners. Dhanarajan & Timmers (1992) support this claim and add that students prefer programs that are

51

suitable, in terms of content and administrative support, for a particular locale; students also prefer study materials that have local applications. However, as pointed out in Section 2.4.5, localisation of programs may be limited by regulatory restrictions.

Related to a particular locale is also the issue of pedagogy that underpins a particular style of instruction; for instance, the pedagogy which supports western style instruction can be very different to that encountered in Asian educational settings (McLoughlin, 2001; Pincas, 2001). Therefore, when developing instruction, it is important to recognise the pedagogical differences between locales and allow for reflective and synergistic learning; classroom interaction may also need to be developed in a different way (Debowski, 2003; Phillips, 1997; Ziguras, 2000).

2.7.3.2. Interaction

Although interaction is a multifaceted concept and can be described to mean different things in a variety of contexts, it is recognised as an important characteristic in instructional design, social context, and success of distance education (Beard & Harper, 2002, Dzakiria 2003). According to Daniel and Marquis, interaction occurs when

> the student is in two-way contact with another person(s) in such a way as to elicit from them reactions and responses which are specific to their own requests and contributions. (Daniel & Marquis, 1983, p. 32)

Interaction underpins the seven principles of good practice in education as established by Chickering & Gamson (1987). These practices include: encouraging contact students and teachers; developing responsiveness and cooperation; engaging in active learning; providing prompt feedback; promoting time on task approach; communicating high expectations; and respecting diversity.

Several aspects of communication have been described in the literature including communication, collaboration, and active learning (Kenny, 2002). The social aspect has also been emphasised (Beard & Harper, 2002; Wagner, 1994). In addition, Web-based interaction has been defined as synchronous (with no time delay) or asynchronous (communication with a delay that allows participants to respond at a later time from when the message is sent) (Smith & Dillon, 1999).

In his definition of interaction Moore (1989) also included the interaction between the learner and the content of the subject of the study, that is learner-content interaction; his typology included three types of interaction: learner-content, learner-instructor, and learner-learner. Moore conceptualised the learner-instructor interaction as interaction both between the learner and the instructional designer, as well as the learner and the teacher. He argued that learner - instructor interaction, *regarded as essential by many educators, and as highly desirable by many learners*, plays a vital role in motivating students to learn, and maintaining and enhancing their interest in subject matter. In addition, he observed that distance learners benefit most from interacting often and in different ways:

> The frequency and intensity of the teacher's influence on learners when there is learner-teacher interaction is much greater than when there is only learner-content interaction. (Moore, 1989)

With respect to learner-learner interaction, Moore (1989) pointed at the importance of peer interaction for distance learners, particularly at the stage of application and evaluation of new content. He also suggested that, particularly for younger learners, *the teaching task of stimulation and motivation will be assisted by peer-group interaction* (Moore, 1989); however, he did not regard this aspect of learner-learner interaction as vital for most adult and advanced learners, as they tend to be self-motivated.

Norman (1998) agreed that interaction in the educational environment occurred along student-teacher, student-student, and student-content lines. He then commented that new technologies enabled designers to take these interactions to new levels.

Hillman, Willis & Gunawardena (1994) highlighted the importance of one more type of interaction, particularly important in online learning: the learner-interface interaction. This interaction occurs between the learner and the technology necessary for online education; a successful online learner must be able to use competently not only the Internet software, but also the basic equipment such as a mouse, keyboard, and printer. Hillman et al. (1994) point out that this may be one of the most challenging types of interaction since it is not required in the traditional classroom.

Jonassen (1985) contended that interactivity requires two-way communication by way of feedback. Clark and Craig (1992) also agreed that provision of student feedback is an integral part of any definition of interactivity.

Effective interaction and feedback is important in meeting individual learner's needs and in providing a forum for suggesting program improvements. More importantly, continuous interaction provides room for learning. Justifying the importance of interaction in distance education, Summers (1991) stated that without interaction teaching would be reduced to *passing on content as if it were dogmatic truth*; he maintained that collaboration between teacher and student, both participating in the role of knowledge acquisition, was needed to enable learners to eventually become independent thinkers. Parker (1999) supported this view, announcing that interaction was an *essential* part of the academic process.

Having investigated the effects of different types of interaction (academic, collaborative, and social) on learning achievement and satisfaction, Jung, Choi, Lim, and Leem (2002) concluded that social interaction with instructors and collaborative interaction with fellow students have significant effects on learning and satisfaction with the program. They also noted that small group activities increased learning motivation. These findings were also supported by Swan (2001) and Hong (2002) who found that student satisfaction and perceived learning correlated with higher perceived levels of interaction with instructors, and fellow students. According to McIsaac, Blocher, Mahes & Vrasidas (1999), students require both structured and informal opportunities to interact with their peers to be satisfied with their program.

Morgan & McKenzie (2003) reported that regular interaction between instructors and students kept the students motivated and on task and prompted them to maintain their study as a high priority among competing obligations; it also contributed to strengthening the students' bond with the university. In addition, the authors highlighted the importance of human support for distance learners as a factor in improving completion rates. Completion rates in distance education tend to be low (Tait & Mills, 2001) and, although affected by many different factors, a weak relationship between student and university plays a major role in student's decision to quit (Garland, 1993; Morgan & Tam, 1999).

In spite of their independence, distance learners still seek the face-to-face interaction with their instructors. Both students and instructors have identified inadequate interaction as one of the biggest frustrations in a distance education program. Keegan (1996) believes that distance learning should strive to recreate the teacher-learner model as an interactive experience. This is substantiated by Sherry when she says:

> The most important factor for successful distance learning is a caring, concerned teacher who is confident, experienced, at ease with the equipment, uses the media creatively, and maintains a high level of interactivity with the students. (Sherry 1996, p. 346)

As supported by many studies, effective distance education is said to revolve around learner-centered teaching styles that decrease psychological distance and increase student participation in the teaching-learning process (Moore & Kearsley, 2005; Verduin & Clark, 1991). Wolcott (1996) suggested *one solution to bridging the psychological distance is to adopt a learner-centered approach to distance teaching* (p. 25). The development of learner-centered skills in course planning, delivery, and evaluation are believed to be essential to effective distance instruction (Belanger & Jordan, 2000; Duffy & Kirkley, 2004; Verduin & Clark, 1991). Effective distance teaching is believed to revolve around a learner-centered system of instruction (Beaudoin, 1990; Dillon & Walsh, 1992) *that demonstrates a bias for direct learner involvement and participation throughout the process* (Ostendorf, 1997, as cited in Dupin-Bryant, 2004, p. 3). Learner-centered distance instructors encourage students to take responsibility for their own learning and focus on facilitation of learning rather than diffusion of information (Duffy & Kirkley, 2004; Granger & Bowman, 2003). The principles of learner-centered distance teaching promote

54

the collaborative, learner-centered teaching styles proclaimed in adult education literature as the most effective way to teach adults (Gibson, 2003; Verduin & Clark, 1991).

Student participation has been singled out by Moore & Kearsley (2005) as one of the most important elements of distance education program design. Regardless of the particular model of a distance education program, students need to be given a chance to ask or answer questions and, in most subjects, need an opportunity to express opinions.

In most distance education programs, students have to submit assignments for evaluation. Prompt meaningful feedback on assignments is very important to students. Most students prefer feedback to be immediate, and they find lack of feedback frustrating. The provision of feedback plays another important role in that it allows instructors to increase students' sense of participation in the program (Carr, 2000; Moore & Kearsley, 2005). Gibbs and Simpson (2004) further observed that in distance education feedback on assignments plays an important dual role: firstly, as the main instrument for teaching; and secondly, as the main means of interaction between student and instructor. Threlkeld & Brzoska (1994) identified one more aspect of the role of timely feedback: it is a critical component of learner support.

2.7.4. The role of technology

Palloff & Pratt (2000) made a point that *technology does not teach students; effective teachers do* (p. 4). They went on to say that the issue is not technology itself, but how it is used in the design and delivery of courses. This view was supported by Macdonald who, in his plenary address at the 11th General Conference: Universities as Gateway to the Future, declared that pedagogy must remain pre-eminent in any educational program:

> Educational technology is a significant supplement, but it does not replace the human element and the qualitative role of the teacher. In all our programmes, there must be a human presence at the end of the line. (Macdonald, 2000)

Advancement in technology does not, in itself, lead to effective distance education. The best distance education practices depend on creative, well-informed instructors (Greenberg, 1998). Bates (1995) suggests that newer technologies are not inherently better than old ones and many of the lessons learned from the application of older technologies will still apply to any newer technology. He again advocates that instructors should draw on their experience and adapt that experience to the new environment of distance learning. The instructors must be trained *not only to use technology, but also to shift the way in which they organise and deliver material* (Palloff & Pratt, 2000, p. 3).

According to Ragan (1999), the process of media selection and application should be guided by three considerations: first, an analysis of the role that the instructional media and supporting tools should play in achieving the learning goals; second, an understanding of the impact of the use of technology; and third, careful consideration of the characteristics of the distance learner. Consequently, the choice of technology should be based upon its ability to support the goals of the learning program, and it should reflect its accessibility to learners; a distance education program should use technology that is appropriate for the widest range of students within that program, is useful, and is easy to use.

The implementation and utilisation of current and emerging technologies offers many potential advantages in achieving educational goals and instructional objectives: it can provide ready access to a vast store of the latest information; it can facilitate communication between students, and students and instructors; and, it can increase student motivation and self-esteem (Hamza & Alhalabi, 1999; Kirkwood 1998; Moore & Kearsley, 2005). However, the advantages to be gained from introducing new technologies into distance education depend on the ability and willingness of the students to use them. Therefore, an assessment of educational needs should be conducted, and potential consequences in the classroom considered, prior to the deployment of those technologies (Hamza & Alhalabi, 1999; Ragan, 1999). Hamza & Alhalabi (1999) also point out the relationship between technology and the culture of an institution. They maintain that, *because technology is a tool, it should never determine how and when the institution's culture should adapt to its existence.* Therefore, the technologies should be aligned with the institution's culture.

Olesinski (1995) highlights the role that technical staff play in distance learning. They not only support the technical delivery of distance programs, but may also indirectly influence the learning environment by *orientating participants to the technology, and reducing the anxiety of the participants* (including the instructor), and by *advising the instructor on instructional techniques* (p. 3). Olesinski found that instructors who were given inadequate orientation to the equipment could not operate it until they had hands-on experience. He pointed out the difference between instructors who could adapt their teaching styles to the technology, and those who could not. Those who adapted were superior in conducting the classes. According to Olesinski, not only do the instructors need to adapt to the educational environment, but they must also adapt to technical staff who can help in the delivery of the educational program. Much of the outcome depends on the attitude of the instructor.

Equipment and hardware malfunctions can be a great detriment to the effectiveness of distance learning. When a problem occurs in a class, everything comes to a standstill and the learning environment is interrupted. Even if an overhead projector goes out during an instructor's presentation, an alternate way of delivering that information may not easily be found. Carter (2001) found that unanticipated technical problems shortened class time and discussion, and that such interruptions negatively affected the overall quality of presentations. Equipment failure can be frustrating for all involved in distance learning. For the instructors, it means that even the best preparation for a class will be lost; for the technician, the frustration and inability to keep the class running smoothly may affect the instructor's view of their competency, causing tension; and, for the student, the inability to feel that progress is being made can hinder the learning process. To counter the adverse effect of equipment malfunction, it has been recommended that alternative modes of delivery be supported in a distance education program, especially one that relies on an *electronic classroom* (Ragan, 1999; Weber, 1996).

2.7.5. The role of program evaluation

Evaluation of a program is important; collecting feedback information from the students sends a message to the students that the instructors and the institution are concerned about their learning, and it also provides the instructor with information useful both for assisting individual students and for making program adjustments. Early evaluation of the program is said to be especially helpful. Chyung et al. (1998) found that satisfaction during the first or second subject of the program was the major factor that decided whether distance learners continued with their program of studies.

Evaluations of program materials and the supporting system are essential in the ongoing process of program monitoring and improvement. Such evaluations reflect students' acceptability of the study materials and the mode of study, and inform the offering institution broadly whether it is meeting students' expectations (Yuen, Timmers, & Chau, 1993).

For successful learning to occur, it is vital to determine what works and what needs to be improved. Evaluation leads to revision of instruction, and revision of instruction helps to achieve the goal of helping students learn (Heinich, Molenda, Russell, & Smaldino, 1996). Eclectic models of evaluation have been advocated by Woodley & Kirkwood (1986), and Sweeney (1995) as most applicable to distance education program evaluation; they recommend the use of both qualitative and quantitative procedures.

One of the crucial inputs in the design and evaluation of distance programs is student feedback. Student feedback assists in identifying the strengths and shortcomings of a curriculum or program and lets the students contribute to the planning and development of their studies (Pratt, 1994; Race, 1994). Moreover, feedback can highlight discrepancies between institutional assumptions and the forms of knowledge, learning styles, aspirations, needs, and values that students bring to the educational context.

Assessment of student satisfaction has been identified as yet another factor contributing to the overall success of a distance education program. Since student satisfaction relates to students' contentedness with several components of a program, it can be used as a measure of its effectiveness (Biner, Dean, & Mellinger, 1994). Biner et al. (1994) argue that high levels of student satisfaction are important because they may contribute to lower program attrition and how much students learn within a distance education program. They conducted two studies to identify major dimensions of learner satisfaction; they identified the following seven dimensions: instructor/instruction, technology, program management, personnel, promptness of material delivery, support services, and out-of-class communication with the instructor. Tallman (1994) agreed that student support services were significantly related to satisfaction, while Gunawardena & Zittle (1997) underlined the role of social presence as a significant contributor to student satisfaction. Interaction was found to be a significant predictor in determining student satisfaction although perceived interaction was found to be as important in predicting satisfaction as actual interaction (Fulford & Zhang, 1993). As student satisfaction can be a measure of program effectiveness, gathering data about student satisfaction with distance education programs may assist in evaluating, planning, and provision of educational services. According to Mazelan, Green, Brannigan, and Tormey:

> Higher education managers who can clearly identify and subsequently measure client-centered quality will be able to capitalize on student-based information to support their claims for resources. (Mazelan et al., 1993, p. 77)

2.7.6. The role of organisational support in the programs

Student support is an important issue associated with the delivery of distance education programs. Student support, while including instructor support of the student related to the course content, also includes support directed to the student's need to access resources traditionally located on campus, such as libraries, registration, and technological assistance in order to access and use web-supported or web-based courses. These support networks are usually in place for the on-campus students. For the distance learner, these support networks are only accessible in a limited way, unless specific measures have been developed to include distance learners. Identifying distance student needs, supporting them through orientations and other support services, understanding the unique communication needs of the distance learner and identifying basic student competencies are all part of providing reasonable levels of distance student support. Khoo & Idrus stated that learners without support are most liable to delay their completion of a programme or drop out altogether. They further say that *without necessary student support services, a distance education programme will not succeed.* (Khoo & Idrus, 2004, p. 1)

Access to library materials has been identified as a key component of distance education (Cavanaugh, 2001; Tait & Mills, 2001). Dillon & Gunawardena (1995) found that access to the institution's library, training on obtaining information through library resources, as well as local library support were significant factors in the successful completion of distance courses. An evaluation of learner support conducted by Dillon, Gunawardena, & Parker in 1992 (cited in Threlkeld & Brzoska, 1994, p. 57) concluded that *library resources are very important to distance students, as the majority of them indicated that success in the course required access to library materials*. In addition, McElhinney & Nasseh (1999) stressed the importance of introducing students to the technology used in the program and giving examples of how it can be best used.

Thorpe (2003) defined student support in a distance education program as *all those elements capable of responding to a known learner or group*. The definition included three key elements: identity, that is the ability to deal with the needs of identifiable individuals; interaction, the ability to be responsive to student needs; and, time/duration, the ability to maintain contact throughout the duration of the program.

Several authors have suggested that student induction and orientation programs are important to introduce students to the institution, the distance learning context, and program requirements. Support for distance learners is needed most at the beginning of the student's involvement with a program when many of the barriers students face need to be overcome including: obtaining information about the program, admission and registration requirements, obtaining study materials, determining workloads and deadlines, and becoming familiar with the technological requirements and instructor expectations (Gibson, 1998, Granger & Benke, 1998, Hardy & Boaz, 1997).

Distance learners may have varying degrees of the necessary skills to successfully complete a distance education program. Granger & Benke suggested ways to decrease the barriers for successful distance learners by keeping administrative processes *simple, convenient, and automatic* by making *both self-help strategies and direct assistance available to aid learners in solving problems as they are encountered*, by providing *back-up materials and systems*, and by continually learning from experiences as an organisation (Granger & Benke, 1998, p. 134).

Peters (1998) pointed out that in addition to providing curriculum and in-text support, helping students deal with administrative or personal problems related to their studies should not be seen as *something that is on the periphery of the learning and teaching process* (p. 62). Simpson (2000) agreed with this view stating further that students want to know that the program providers care and show commitment; this includes supportive local staff, a dedicated program coordinator, and quick response to queries and complaints. He went on to say that the better the support, the better students perform and the more satisfied they are in the program; they are also more likely to show understanding and continue with the program when, inevitably, mistakes are made (Simpson, 2000).

Shin (2003) found that the view that a student holds about the institution offering the program has a significant effect on performance and satisfaction; the view is shaped by the quality of institutional support including student services, availability of resources, and technical support. To this end, the program coordinator plays a significant dual role: focusing on customer service and quality control. Referring to transnational programs in particular, Debowski (2003) pointed out that, as the key contact for both students and offshore partners, the coordinator needs to be able to respond quickly and effectively to queries, problems and complaints.

Reputation of the offering institution and quality of the program are important to transnational students, particularly in Asia where reputation is a major selling point to potential students (Debowski, 2003). Program providers must therefore ensure that the reputation of the institution remains intact, and that the standards of the transnational program parallel those required of students in similar programs offered at home (Biggs, 2001; Van Damme, 2001). To ensure high quality of transnational programs, universities need to develop a range of strategies to build and maintain these standards; first, they need to clearly formulate and communicate the underlying curriculum philosophy and practices; second, they need to provide learning opportunities that can be adapted to the need of offshore students, while still reflecting the overall standards established by the providing university; thirdly, assessments need to be moderated to uphold standards; and, lastly, learning materials need to be regularly updated to maintain their relevance and accuracy in a fast changing educational context (Biggs, 2001; Debowski, 2003).

2.8. CONCLUSION

Distance education programs have evolved considerably from the inception of the first correspondence courses in 1840 to the many types of present distance delivery modalities. The rapid expansion of distance education offerings is providing students with more options; good quality programs will be demanded. This great increase in the number of distance education programs, students, and providers has prompted researchers to investigate the effectiveness of such programs.

The characteristics of effective distance education programs to be used in this research study emerged from the comprehensive review of literature. Numerous studies have determined the attributes of effective distance education through the attributes of its components including: students, instructors, program design, technologies, and organisational support. Literature sources dealing with predictors of successful distance students revealed that those students experienced satisfactory levels of communication with the instructors and good quality teaching.

Research related to students' perceptions has focused on identifying factors related to satisfaction, attitudes, and perceived learning and interaction. Factors affecting satisfaction are often considered to be organisational and involve the learning environment, program management, and support services: they are identifiable factors that relate to distance students' perceptions about the effectiveness of their learning experiences.

Knowledge of the characteristics of effective distance education programs may assist students, staff, and institutions in making informed decisions regarding such programs; students will be better informed when deciding to enroll; staff, when working on design and development; institutions when considering deployment of distance education programs. Development of a model for effective distance programs to provide a framework upon which decisions about such programs could be made has been the motivation for this research study.

Chapter 3 discusses the approach used to develop and validate a model for effective distance education programs.

Chapter 3

RESEARCH METHODS

3.1. INTRODUCTION

Chapter 2 provided a review of literature in five areas related to the present study, including: the evolution of distance education; the impact of technology on distance education; the transnational education model; requirements of computing education at a distance; and, distance education effectiveness. This review of literature provided guidance in the development of this investigation. This chapter goes on to discuss the approach used to develop and validate the multidimensional model for transnational education programs; it describes the research design, the population and sample, instrumentation, data collection, and data analyses that were used in the study. Section 3.2 describes methods used in the development and validation of the multidimensional model. Section 3.3 provides a description of data sources used for validation. Section 3.4 describes the means by which the data was collected. Section 3.5 discusses ethical considerations associated with data collection, and Section 3.6 describes the methods used for the analysis of data.

3.2. RESEARCH PROCEDURES

This research study had multiple goals: first, to identify from literature success attributes of distance education programs; second, based on the identified attributes, to develop a model for successful distance education programs (with emphasis on transnational programs); and third, to validate the model against selected transnational programs. This section describes the methods used in the development and validation of the model.

3.2.1. Development of the multidimensional model

This research study set out to develop a conceptual model for effective transnational education programs: a model that would help to determine why a particular program is effective. To this end, it was important to identify the specific attributes that optimise the effectiveness of distance education programs including transnational programs.

Literature suggested attributes contributing to the quality and effectiveness of distance education programs. However, a great majority of the literature sources related to online distance education programs and students, other types of technology-based programs, and traditional correspondence programs. This study needed to identify attributes applicable to transnational programs: programs that are supported by technology, but include a substantial face-to-face component. Consequently, the review of literature was a two-step process: first, general attributes contributing to the effectiveness of distance education programs were identified; and second, these attributes were assessed in terms of their relevance to transnational programs – only the applicable attributes were selected for consideration in the model. As a result, a final set of attributes was determined. The attributes related to various aspects of the transnational education context including: learners, instructors, program design, technology, evaluation and assessment, and organisational support. Next, in accordance with the bottom-up approach for model development adopted in this study, these attributes were grouped into broader categories – dimensions – describing distinctive aspects of transnational education programs. This collection of dimensions formed a model of effective transnational programs. Details of the model are presented in Chapter 4.

3.2.2. Validation of the model

Following its development, the model was applied to three transnational computing programs for validation; the validation aimed to determine how the multiple dimensions of the model were apparent in those programs, and if some of the individual characteristics within each dimension were more important to students than others.

This research study employed both qualitative and quantitative methods of evaluation. The qualitative method of evaluation was chosen to complement the quantitative method. Quantitative methods alone often tend to focus on parts of the whole, leading to the investigation of potentially isolated, out-of-context, and unrelated parts (Patton, 1987). On the other hand, qualitative methods focus on providing description and understanding of an entire program or selected aspects of it as a whole (Firestone, 1987). This feature of qualitative evaluation was important to this study as it aimed to identify how success attributes manifest themselves in an entire transnational program. In order to determine the influence of various program attributes, data was collected from participating students through quantitative surveys and qualitative group interviews.

Quantitative surveys were conducted with participants to attain representative answers; these surveys were conducted via questionnaires with closed questions, and the data was then analysed to give statistically significant results. The questionnaires were used to allow participants to note which elements of the learning experience contributed to, or limited, their satisfaction with the program; they were also used to measure the perceived importance of program attributes with respect to program effectiveness. The collected information allowed in-depth examination of the content, structure and process of the evaluated programs (Chute et al., 1999; Wisher & Curnow, 1998).

A self-completion questionnaire was chosen as the most suitable format of the survey instrument for this study because first, it is an effective research tool for small scale studies; second, it enabled the collection of data in a relatively quick and inexpensive manner; and third, *because the knowledge needed is controlled by the questions, therefore it affords a good deal of precision and clarity* (McDonough & McDonough, 1997, p. 171). In addition, data collected through questionnaires was likely to be more *uniform* and *accurate* than that obtained by other methods as respondents completed the questionnaires under the condition of anonymity and therefore provided more honest replies (Seliger & Shohamy, 2000, p. 172).

In addition to surveys, qualitative group interviews with a smaller number of students were used as a further mechanism to discuss factors perceived as critical to the effectiveness of distance education programs; they were also used to seek elaboration on issues that arose from survey responses. According to Chute et al. (1999), qualitative research enables the exploration of a specific object as deeply as possible. Therefore, the number of participants is smaller and interviews are less formally structured. The interviews typically involve open-ended questions resulting in 'rich' data, which requires more analysis and input by the researchers. Although group interviews are more time-consuming than questionnaires, they provide an opportunity to interact with the students and clarify issues (Chute et al., 1999).

3.3. DATA SOURCES

Three transnational computing programs were selected to validate the multidimensional model for effective transnational computing education. All three programs were delivered offshore in Hong Kong by Australian universities in co-operation with Hong Kong partner institutions. It must be noted that to protect the anonymity and the privacy of Australian universities and their transnational partners, as well as participants of group interviews, no specific information is provided in this thesis regarding the location, or name of individuals or institutions.

The transnational computing programs selected for evaluation included: Program 1, Bachelor of Business (Computer Systems Support) degree – BBCS, offered by Australian university, University A, together with a Hong Kong partner institution, Partner A. The program commenced in 1997, and has produced over a hundred graduates to date; Program 2, Bachelor of Computer Science degree – BCO, also offered by University A, but with a different Hong Kong partner, Partner B. This program has operated since 1992 and has graduated over two thousand students; and, Program 3, Bachelor of Information Technology degree – BIT, offered by a different university, University B, in cooperation with the same Hong Kong partner as Program 2 (Partner B). Program 3 commenced in 1999 and has graduated nearly four hundred students to date. Table 3.3 depicts the affiliation of the selected programs with their respective universities and Hong Kong partners.

Table 3.3. Affiliation of the evaluated programs.

Program ID	Program Type	Australian University	Hong Kong Partner
Program 1	Bachelor of Business (Computer Systems Support)	A	A
Program 2	Bachelor of Computer Science	A	B
Program 3	Bachelor of Information Technology	B	B

The programs operated in part-time mode for students who had previous approved tertiary qualifications. Students were normally in full-time employment, and usually studied six subjects per year – two subjects per term. In each of the programs, lecturers from Australia were responsible for the design of curriculum, detailed teaching plans, continuous and final assessment, as well as face-to-face delivery of twenty five percent of the program. Part-time local lecturers taught the remaining part of the program. All programs relied on the Internet for communication and provision of study material, e.g. subject Web sites, bulletin boards, and email. Students met with lecturers and fellow students through face-to-face sessions, and benefited from Web based support between sessions.

3.4. DATA COLLECTION INSTRUMENTS AND STRATEGIES

Data collection for the study included a survey and group interviews with students. Since surveys are considered the core methodology for gaining data on individuals' opinions or preferences, a survey was selected as a suitable data collection instrument for this study; the survey included both quantitative and qualitative components. In addition to the survey, group interviews with students were held to further discuss factors perceived as critical to the effectiveness of distance education programs and clarify questions that arose from survey responses.

3.4.1. Survey

The purpose of the survey evaluation was twofold: to determine which aspects of multiple dimensions of transnational programs were perceived by students as most important to the effectiveness of such programs; and, to assess the extent of students' satisfaction with the various dimensions of their current programs.

3.4.1.1. Survey design

In accordance with its dual purpose, the survey (Appendix A) included two main sections; section B, developed by the researcher, was based on the dimensions and characteristics of the multidimensional model and designed to determine the perceived importance of the various characteristics to program effectiveness; and, section A, adapted from a published survey (Biner, 1993), was used to measure students' satisfaction with their current programs.

Section B of the survey was composed of ten tables representing the dimensions of the developed model; each dimension included a list of characteristics (in no particular order). In each of the dimensions, students were asked to select only three characteristics that, in their opinion, contributed to program effectiveness, and rank the selected characteristics in order of importance. This section also included further descriptive questions aimed at establishing the effectiveness of the transnational program model (that is, one inclusive of a face-to-face component), and determining student preferences regarding possible fully online provision of such programs.

Section A of the survey was designed to measure students' satisfaction with their current programs. An extensive search was conducted to locate a published survey. For research in the academic environment, a majority of the scholars used the Likert scale Teleconference Evaluation Questionnaire (TEQ) developed by Paul Biner (1993). The TEQ, which was specifically developed for measuring student satisfaction in a classroom using interactive teleconference video, was tested by Biner (1993), and found to be very reliable. Consequently, the TEQ was selected and adapted for the purpose of this study.

The modifications to the original TEQ were twofold: first, questions pertaining to the teleconference characteristics of the program were eliminated from the questionnaire; and second, additional questions pertaining to transnational programs were included. It should be noted that modified versions of the TEQ have been used in other studies; for instance, Galante (1997) adapted the TEQ to measure satisfaction levels of students in a traditional program; similarly, Ricketts, Irani, & Jones (2003) modified the TEQ for traditional on-campus students by removing specific questions pertaining to distance education.

3.4.1.2. Pilot test

The initial form of the survey was administered to a group of students (N=12) in Program 2. Students were asked to respond to survey items and also comment regarding the survey's readability and ambiguity, if any. All twelve students completed the survey and responded with comments.

After the pilot test, minor wording changes were made to clarify directions regarding completion of the survey and reduce the ambiguity of one item; item 12 in Section B was changed from "Is this type of course worthwhile? Why?" to "Is this type of course (offered by an offshore university) worthwhile? Why?"

The pilot study served two purposes: (1) to test the layout of the instrument, and (2) to utilise transnational students to obtain feedback on item clarity. The pilot study was important because it confirmed the ease of following the survey instructions, and the clarity of survey items. In addition, the pilot survey provided information regarding the approximate length of time students would need to complete the survey.

3.4.1.3. Survey – data collection

All students invited to participate in the survey were in the final year of their degree programs. The choice of final year participants was based on the need for the participants to have experienced all aspects of a transnational program.

Students were asked during one of their lectures by a non-lecturer to complete the questionnaire, which was handed to them with a plain return envelope; a cover sheet including information about the survey was provided as part of the questionnaire (Appendix B). The students were asked to either complete the questionnaire during the lecture, or take it away and return it later to a drop-in box provided in a convenient location; the survey took approximately twenty minutes to complete; and, participation in completing the survey was voluntary and anonymous.

The survey was administered to approximately three hundred students in the selected programs in July and August 2003. Two-hundred-and-fifty-nine useable completed surveys were returned (86% response rate). The breakdown of useable survey numbers across the programs is presented in Table 3.4.1.3.

Table 3.4.1.3. Useable survey numbers in the evaluated programs.

Program ID	Australian University	Hong Kong Partner	Number of surveys
Program 1	A	A	53
Program 2	A	B	161
Program 3	B	B	45

3.4.2. Group interviews with students

Following a preliminary analysis of survey data, group interviews were held with students from each of the three participating programs. Questions asked were designed to clarify and deepen the researcher's understanding of the program characteristics that students perceived as critical to program effectiveness. The sequence of data collection (analysis of survey results followed by interviews) provided an opportunity for the researcher to determine if issues arose from the surveys that needed to be clarified or further discussed.

The analysis of survey results revealed that there were differences in students' responses based on the particular program in which they were enrolled. Hence, one of the questions asked during the interviews was, "What is it like to be a student in this program?" This question was followed by a related question: "To what extent does this program meet your expectations?" One other issue that called for clarification was the students' perceived opposition to fully online provision of the program; hence, the following question was asked: "Would you prefer the course to be fully online, or face-to-face, why?" The remainder of the questions for the interviews were developed to broaden the researcher's understanding of the programs. A summary of group interview procedures and questions is presented in the Group Interviews Guide included in Appendix C.

Students were invited to take part in the group interviews through email; announcements were also posted on the relevant program Web sites (Appendix D). Students, who volunteered to participate in the group interviews, were sent a copy of the consent form (Appendix E). Students were subsequently reminded individually of the scheduled dates and times of the interviews through email.

The group interviews with students were conducted over a period of two weeks in December 2003. Each interview session lasted approximately one hour. A total of forty-four students participated in six group interviews with the breakdown of student numbers across the programs presented in Table 3.4.2.

Table 3.4.2. Student participation in group interviews.

Program ID	Australian University	Hong Kong Partner	Number of interview participants
Program 1	A	A	7 (1 session)
Program 2	A	B	29 (4 sessions)
Program 3	B	B	8 (1 session)

In order to minimise researcher bias, each interview had an outside facilitator. The facilitator was provided with an outline of the discussion to be held during the session. This guide included an introduction, a suggested warm-up question, a list of key questions, and a summary (Greenbaum, 1998); each interview session followed the same process. The researcher served as a note-taker along with one other note taker. Following each interview session, the researcher, the facilitator, and the additional note-taker held a meeting to analyse and interpret student responses and compare notes. The notes were analysed for themes that supported results of the survey, themes that differed from the survey results, and new themes that emerged. Data was also analysed for additional characteristics and dimensions that were not included in the multidimensional model, but were identified by the students as factors that impacted on the program.

3.5. ETHICAL CONSIDERATIONS

Permission was obtained from the Human Research Ethics Committee at Victoria University to conduct this study on "Critical Success Characteristics in Offshore Computing Programs". Appendix F provides a copy of the approval letter. The consenting adults participating in this study were at minimal risk. However, participants were informed in writing of the purpose and duration of the research, the benefits of participation, and the extent of confidentiality of records identifying the participants. An explanation of whom to contact for answers to pertinent questions about the research and a statement that participation was voluntary were also included (Appendices D and E).

3.6. DATA ANALYSIS

The process of data collection and analysis was designed to validate the multidimensional model by determining:

(a) the level of students' satisfaction with the attributes of the current program;

(b) which attributes within each dimension were ranked by the students as most important to the success of their program;

(c) if any of the attributes were perceived by the students as most important across all dimensions;

(d) if other attributes, currently not included in the model, were identified by the students as critical to the effectiveness of the program.

The statistical analyses were conducted using the SPSS version 12.0. Descriptive statistics were used to summarise the results of student surveys. Independent samples T-test was used to compare, in terms of student satisfaction, programs offered by the same university, and programs offered in cooperation with the same Hong Kong partner. Where the data did not conform to the assumptions of the normal distribution, non-parametric statistical tests were chosen for the analysis of the data. In particular, Wilcoxon test for paired data was carried out to determine statistical significance of student satisfaction with University and Hong Kong (local) instructors in each of the evaluated programs. An alpha level of 0.05 was used to determine the level of significance for this study.

To analyse the perceived importance of program attributes within dimensions, reverse weighting of top three attributes was used. This enabled simple, namely based on a single value, ranking of attributes within a dimension. The first, second, and third preferences were weighted as follows: first preference was assigned a weight of 3, second preference – weight of 2, third preference – weight of 1, and lack of preference – weight of 0. The overall importance of an attribute within a dimension was obtained from the sum of the weighted student preferences for that attribute in the dimension.

Content analysis was used to analyse the transcribed data of the group interviews with students. The data was reduced to themes and then interpreted. The four themes that emerged from the analysis included: factors influencing students' decision about enrolling in a transnational program; students' perceptions regarding program effectiveness; their views on potential fully online provision of the program; and, suggestions for program improvement.

Following the analyses of survey results and notes from interviews, the results from both sources were analysed further and related to each of the dimensions of the model. Similarities, differences, relationships, and new themes as well as unexpected developments were examined. The research findings are reported in Chapter 4, according to the nine hypotheses developed for this study in Chapter 1 (Section 1.2). In addition, other pertinent findings gathered throughout the course of this research study were also reported.

3.7. CONCLUSION

This chapter presents the approach used to develop and validate the multidimensional model for transnational education programs; it describes the research design, the population and sample, instrumentation, data collection, and data analyses that were used in this research study.

The development of the multidimensional model was a two-step process. Firstly, success characteristics of distance education programs, with emphasis on transnational programs, were identified. Secondly, these characteristics were grouped into broader categories – dimensions – describing distinctive aspects of transnational education programs. This collection of dimensions formed a model of effective transnational programs.

To validate the conceptual model and provide responses to the hypotheses of this study, two methods of data collection and multiple data sources were used. The methods included a survey and group interviews, and the sources included three transnational computing programs. The survey focused on the perceived satisfaction with the current program, as well as the perceived importance of program attributes with regard to the effectiveness of transnational education programs. The group interviews served as a complementary source of pertinent information about critical success attributes of transnational programs.

Chapter 4 presents and describes the proposed multidimensional model for transnational education programs, detailing the dimensions of the model together with their attributes; reports the results of model validation through the survey and group interviews with students; and, presents the refined version of the model following validation.

Chapter 4

COMPOSITION, VALIDATION AND REFINEMENT OF THE MULTIDIMENSIONAL MODEL

4.1. INTRODUCTION

Chapter 3 described methods used in the development of the multidimensional model for transnational education programs; it also described the field-testing component of the validation of the model. This chapter goes on to present the conclusion to the development and validation of the model by, first, detailing the dimensions of the model together with their attributes in Section 4.2; second, describing the transnational computing education programs used for validation of the model in Section 4.3; third, presenting the results of model validation through the survey (Section 4.4) and group interviews with students (Section 4.5); and, finally, presenting the refined version of the model following validation in Section 4.6. This chapter also provides responses to the research hypotheses tested in this study.

4.2. THE MULTIDIMENSIONAL MODEL

The study involved the development of a conceptual model for effective transnational education programs. The development of the model was carried out in two stages: (1) identification and investigation of the particular attributes that increase the effectiveness of distance education programs; and, (2) proposal of a model for such programs based on these attributes by grouping the attributes into broader categories – dimensions. The dimensions described distinctive aspects of the programs including student, instructor, curriculum, interaction, technology, assessment, and program management. The derived dimensions formed the proposed model for effective transnational programs.

4.2.1. Development of dimensions

A comprehensive review of the literature, reported in Chapter 2, revealed a number of attributes that contribute to the effectiveness of distance education programs. These attributes were first identified from the literature (Chapter 2, Section 2.7), then examined and grouped into eight broader dimensions to form the multidimensional model; these dimensions, presented in Figure 4.2.1, include *Student, Instructor and learning environment, Instructor – Technology and organisation, Curriculum and instruction design, Interaction, Evaluation and assessment, Technology,* and *Program management and organisational support.*

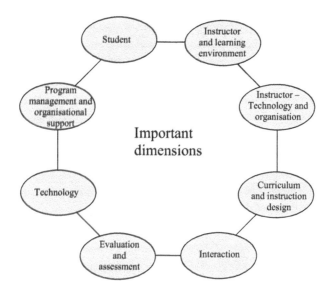

Figure 4.2.1. Proposed dimensions of the multidimensional model.

Since transnational education programs involve both university instructors as well as instructors of the partner institutions in Hong Kong, dimensions *Instructor and learning environment* and *Instructor – Technology and organisation* were further divided into *University instructor and learning environment* and *Hong Kong instructor and learning environment*, and *University instructor – Technology and support* and *Hong Kong instructor – Technology and support* respectively; this extension of the two instructor-related dimensions was motivated by the need to distinguish between the effectiveness of instructors from the offering university and the partner institution. While a similar argument could be presented with respect to dimensions *Interaction*, *Evaluation and assessment*, and *Course management and organisational support*, the roles of the instructors overarch these dimensions and splitting those dimensions along the university/partner institution lines was considered to be of limited benefit.

4.2.2. Dimensions and their attributes

The derived dimensions together with their defining attributes are presented in tables 4.2.2.a through to 4.2.2.h. Table 4.2.2.a presents the details of the dimension *Student* including references to literature.

Table 4.2.2.a. Attributes of the dimension: *Student.*

Attribute	Literature references
Works as a team player.	Burge, 1994; Hardy & Boaz, 1997;
Has positive attitude towards technology-based learning.	Bajtelsmit, 1998; Chyung et al., 1998; Fahy & Archer, 1999; Lim, 2001; Neal, 1999; Simonson et al., 2000; Stein, 1998.
Is motivated and self-disciplined.	Billings, 1998; Granger & Benke, 1998; Kember, 1995; Morgan & Tam, 1999; Saba, 2000.
Is confident in using technology.	Bajtelsmit, 1998; Christensen et al., 2001; Irons et al., 2002; Valentine, 2002.
Knows how to work independently.	Burge, 1994; Kember, 1995; Parker, 1997; Saba, 2000.
Is involved and participates.	Burge, 1994; Hardy & Boaz, 1997.
Is willing to ask instructors for assistance.	Bernt & Bugbee, 1993; Brown, 1998.

In general, the literature points out that successful distance education students need to be motivated and determined; they need to be positive about technology and willing to participate.

The second dimension in the model is the *Instructor and learning environment* dimension. Table 4.2.2.b presents the details of this dimension together with literature references.

Table 4.2.2.b. Attributes of the dimension: *Instructor and learning environment.*

Attribute	Literature references
Understands course requirements, students' characteristics and needs.	Carter, 2001; Granger & Benke, 1998; McLoughlin, 2001; Omoregie, 1997; Pincas, 2001.
Encourages students to take responsibility for their own learning.	Duffy & Kirkley, Granger & Bowman, 2003; 2004; Hiltz & Wellman, 1997; Ostendorf, 1997; Saba, 2000.
Encourages communication between students, and students and instructors.	Moore & Kearsley, 2005; Morgan & McKenzie, 2003; Palloff & Pratt, 1999.
Demonstrates dedication to course, teaching and students.	Carr, 2000; Carter, 2001; Frew & Webber, 1995; Inman & Kerwin, 1999; Roblyer & Wiencke, 2003; Sherry, 1996; Stark & Warne, 1999.
Uses effective communication skills.	Moore & Kearsley, 2005.
Conducts students' needs assessment and course evaluation.	Fahy & Archer, 1999; Granger & Benke, 1998.
Ensures students' support services.	Palloff & Pratt, 1999; Stark & Warne, 1999.

Overall, according to the literature, instructors involved in distance education programs need to be good communicators dedicated to students and teaching; they need to encourage communication between students, and between students and instructors. They also need to carry out needs assessment program evaluation.

The next dimension is also related to the instructor but, in this case, it is the instructor in the role of a designer and manager. Table 4.2.2.c presents the details of the dimension *Instructor – Technology and organisation* including references to literature.

Table 4.2.2.c. Attributes of the dimension: *Instructor – Technology and organisation.*

Attribute	Literature references
Has positive attitude towards technology.	Sherry, 1996; Weber, 1996.
Demonstrates control over technology.	Carr, 2000; Debowski, 2003; Weber, 1996.
Adapts course materials for delivery through electronic media.	Debowski, 2003; Olesinski, 1995; Schauer et al., 1998; Schweb et al., 1998; Sherry, 1996.
Has experience with technology-based courses.	Carr, 2000; Sherry, 1996.
Is well prepared and organised.	Carr, 2000; Wilkes & Burnham, 1991.
Is proficient in instructional design.	Schauer et al., 1998; Schweb et al., 1998.
Uses interactive instructional strategies.	Debowski, 2003; Morgan & McKenzie, 2003; Phillips, 1997; Schauer et al., 1998.
Provides well-designed syllabus and presentation outlines.	Egan et al., 1991; Palloff & Pratt, 1999.
Develops effective graphics.	McLoughlin, 2001; Ouyang & Fu, 1996; Pincas, 2001.

To summarise these attributes, the literature points out that an effective distance education embraces and promotes the use of technology, and possesses strong skills in instructional design.

The next dimension includes the attributes related to distance program design including curriculum and the design of instruction. Table 4.2.2.d presents the details of the dimension *Curriculum and instruction* design including references to literature.

Table 4.2.2.d. Attributes of the dimension: *Curriculum and instruction design.*

Attribute	Literature references
Relates the new material to previous student knowledge.	Buchanan, 2000; Willis, 1995.
Integrates all course elements into a well-paced package.	Moore & Kearsley, 2005.
Is relevant to job/career.	Capper, 1999; Dhanarajan & Timmers, 1992; Moore & Kearsley, 2005; Simon, 1994.
Creates logical sequences for each element presented.	Buchanan, 2000; Olson, 1991;
Course objectives and learning outcomes are communicated to students.	Freeman & Capper, 1999; Palloff & Pratt, 1999.
Instructors and students agree on deadlines for completion and marking of assignments.	Hara & Kling, 1999; Palloff & Pratt, 1999.
Learning objectives are supported by instructional methodologies.	Freeman & Capper, 1999; McLoughlin, 2001; Pincas, 2001; Ragan, 1999.

To sum up, the literature highlights the need for the distance program curriculum to be relevant to the students' jobs and careers, form a well-structured learning unit, and to be well integrated with the students' past knowledge and experience. The design of program instruction needs to reflect program objectives, and involve students in the setting of deadlines. Students also need to be made aware of program objectives and requirements.

Interaction is the next dimension. Its attributes identified from literature are presented in Table 4.2.2.e.

Table 4.2.2.e. Attributes of the dimension: *Interaction.*

Attribute	Literature references
Timely feedback on assignments and projects.	Carr, 2000; Gibbs & Simpson, 2004; Hara & Kling, 1999; Moore & Kearsley, 2005; Palloff & Pratt, 1999.
Involvement in small learning groups.	Gibson, 2003; Hong, 2002; Jung et al., 2002; Swan, 2001; Verduin & Clark, 1991.
Use of interactive instructional strategies.	McIsaac et al., 1999; Moore & Kearsley, 2005.
Frequent contact with the instructor.	Moore & Kearsley, 2005; Morgan & McKenzie, 2003.
Use of electronic media and telephone to interact with instructors.	Bernt & Bugbee, 1993; Hong, 2002; Howell & Jayaratna, 2000.
Development of formats and strategies encouraging communication between students, and students and instructors.	Beard & Harper, 2003; Debowski, 2003; Dzakiria, 2003; Jung et al., 2002; McIsaac et al., 1999; McLoughlin; 2001; Morgan & Tam, 1999; Phillips, 1997; Pincas, 2001.

Overall, the literature points out the importance of timely feedback on assessment tasks and frequent and versatile interaction between students, and students and instructors.

The next dimension is *Evaluation and assessment*. The details of this dimension are presented in Table 4.2.2.f.

Table 4.2.2.f. Attributes of the dimension: *Evaluation and assessment.*

Attribute	Literature references
Assessment of students' attitudes and levels of satisfaction.	Biner et al., 1994; Chyung et al., 1998; Heinich et al., 1996; Mazelan et al., 1993; Pratt, 1994; Sweeney, 1995; Tallman, 1994.
Assessment of the relevance of course content in practice.	Capper, 1999; Yuen et al., 1993.
Methods of assessment match learning objectives.	Freeman & Capper, 1999; Heinich et al., 1996; Yuen et al., 1993.
Continuous evaluation of students' academic progress.	Heinich et al., 1996; Pratt, 1994; Race, 1994.
Continuous evaluation of the course.	Chyung et al., 1998; Heinich et al., 1996; Sweeney, 1995; Woodley & Kirkwood, 1996; Yuen et al., 1993.

To summarise these attributes, the literature indicates the need to conduct various methods of student, subject, and program assessment.

Technology is the next dimension. Table 4.2.2.g presents the details of this dimension including references to literature.

Table 4.2.2.g. Attributes of the dimension: *Technology.*

Attribute	Literature references
Current products are used.	Hamza & Alhalabi, 1999; Kirkwood 1998; Moore & Kearsley, 2005.
Is helpful and easy to use.	Carter, 2001; Ragan, 1999.
Is available and reliable.	Carter, 2001; Palloff & Pratt, 1999; Ragan, 1999.
Software applications are appropriate and easy to use.	Ragan, 1999.
Access to technical assistance throughout the course.	Granger & Benke, 1998; Khoo & Idrus, 2004; Ragan, 1999; Shin, 2003.

According to literature, the technology used in a distance education program needs to be current and easy to use; it also needs to be dependable, with technical help readily available in case of failure.

The final dimension covers the organisational and administrative aspects of a distance education program. The details of the dimension *Program management and organisational support* are presented in Table 4.2.2.h.

Table 4.2.2.h. Attributes of the dimension: *Program management and organisational support.*

Attribute	Literature references
Timely preparation of course materials.	Frew & Webber, 1995; Inman & Kerwin, 1999.
Procedures exist to quickly respond to student complaints.	Debowski, 2003; Granger & Benke, 1998; Khoo & Idrus, 2004; Peters, 1998; Simpson, 2000.
Institution ensures high quality of the course.	Biggs, 2001; Debowski, 2003; Frew & Webber, 1995; Inman & Kerwin, 1999; Shin, 2003; Thorpe, 2003; Van Damme, 2001.
Student support services are provided (e.g. student registration, distribution of materials, ordering of textbooks, processing of examination results).	Gibson b, 1998; Granger & Benke, 1998; Hardy & Boaz, 1997; Khoo & Idrus, 2004; Palloff & Pratt, 1999; Shin, 2003.
Training on obtaining information through course Web sites, electronic databases, interlibrary loans, etc. provided.	Dillon & Gunawardena, 1995; Khoo & Idrus, 2004; McElhinney & Nasseh, 1999.
Effective overall course coordination.	Granger & Benke, 1998; Peters, 1998; Simpson, 2000; Thorpe, 2003.

In short, the literature points out that student support, planning, good coordination and quality control mechanisms are of vital importance to the effectiveness of a distance education program.

4.3. TRANSNATIONAL PROGRAMS CONSIDERED IN THE STUDY

Three transnational computing programs, which are offered in Hong Kong by Australian universities, in co-operation with Hong Kong partner institutions, were selected for evaluation of the multidimensional model. Program1, Bachelor of Business (Computer Systems Support) degree – BBCS, is offered by an Australian university, University A, together with a Hong Kong partner institution, Partner A. The program commenced in 1997, and has produced over one hundred graduates to date. Program2, Bachelor of Computer Science degree – BCO, is also offered by University A, but with a different Hong Kong partner, Partner B. This program has operated since 1992 and has graduated over two thousand students. The third program, Program3, Bachelor of Information Technology degree – BIT, has been offered by a different university, University B, in cooperation with the same Hong Kong partner as Program 2 (Partner B). Program 3 commenced in 1999 and has graduated nearly four hundred students to date.

The Australian universities, University A and University B, offering the programs considered in this study, have the same organisational profile: that is, they are 'mixed mode' institutions, as defined by Rumble (1986) and Holmberg (1995). According to this definition, a mixed mode institution has one of the following organisational profiles: (1) responsibility for organisation may rest with a single department within the institution, with the institution responsible for administration; or, (2) departments may be responsible for both organisation and administration of their own programs; or, (3) a dedicated unit within the organisation may offer distance education in a variety of disciplines and be solely devoted to this purpose. University A and University B both fall into the second category that is, the transnational programs offered by these universities are managed and administered by departments; those departments also deliver the programs to on-campus students in Australia.

The transnational programs considered in this study all meet the definition of a 'twinning program' as defined by McBurnie & Pollock (1998). This means that the programs are fully taught programs and they follow the same syllabus and timetable as the corresponding home campus programs. The offshore students follow the same study materials, assessment tasks, and examinations as home campus students in the offering institution. The provider institution also participates in selecting local academic staff. A detailed discussion on the typology of transnational education programs is presented in Section 2.4.2.

From a technological perspective, all three evaluated programs meet Taylor's (2001) definition of a fourth generation, that is Flexible Learning Model, in that Internet is the main supporting technology in all the programs. The technological classification of the evaluated programs can be further narrowed down by using Gallagher's (2001) three-type categorisation; in this categorisation the types vary with respect to their dependence on the Internet. According to this categorisation, all the evaluated programs fall into the Web Supplemented category. Finally, the Web Supplemented categorisation of the programs can be further refined as Informational and Supplemental (Meares, 2001); Informational as the on-line component serves as an optional source of general program information, for example program outline; and, Supplemental as the on-line component complements other forms of instruction, for example it contains lecture notes. A detailed discussion of technology based models referred to in this paragraph is presented in Section 2.3.3.

All the evaluated programs operate in part-time mode for students who are normally in full-time employment. Students have previous approved tertiary qualifications and, depending on the type of the qualifications, are required to complete between ten and twelve subjects to graduate. The subjects are offered over three terms a year; students usually study two subjects per term – a total of six subjects per year. Classes are held at night, starting at 6:30pm, during the week, and in the afternoon on Saturdays; classes are held at a venue provided by the Hong Kong partner institution. Classes for a single subject are held once a week with the exception of times when Australian lecturers come to Hong Kong to teach; then, for logistical purposes, classes are held more often – for example three classes might be delivered over a period of ten days. While the scheduled classes are face-to-face sessions, students benefit from Web based support between sessions.

In all the evaluated programs, University lecturers from Australia are responsible for the design of curriculum, provision of detailed weekly teaching plans and study materials for each subject in the program, design and provision of continuous and final assessment tasks, as well as face-to-face delivery of twenty five-percent of the program. Part-time local (Hong Kong) lecturers, associated with the partner institutions, teach the remaining part of the program following the teaching plans provided by the University lecturers. In addition to the face-to-face component, the program relies on the Internet for communication, for example subject Web sites, bulletin boards, and email.

In this study, the purpose of the evaluation was twofold: to assess the extent of students' satisfaction with the multiple dimensions of their program, and to determine which aspects of these dimensions were perceived by students as most important to the effectiveness of the program. Data was collected through a survey administered to approximately three hundred students in the selected programs in July and August 2003. Two hundred and fifty nine useable completed surveys were returned. In addition, group interviews with students were conducted to clarify any issues that may have arisen from the survey; forty-four students participated in six group interviews. Table 4.3 presents the breakdown of survey and group interviews numbers across the evaluated programs; details of programs' affiliation with their respective Australian universities and partner institutions in Hong Kong are also included in the table.

Table 4.3. Student participation in survey and group interviews.

Program ID	Program Type	Australian University	Hong Kong Partner	Number of surveys	Number of interview participants
Program 1	Bachelor of Business (Computer Systems Support)	A	A	53	7 (1 session)
Program 2	Bachelor of Computer Science	A	B	161	29 (4 sessions)
Program 3	Bachelor of Information Technology	B	B	45	8 (1 session)

The following section (Section 4.4) presents the results of model validation through the survey, while Section 4.5 discusses the results of group interviews with the students. Finally, following the validation, the refined version of the multidimensional model is presented in section 4.6.

80

4.4. SURVEY RESULTS

Students enrolled in the final year of the targeted programs were invited to complete a survey. For each of the targeted programs, the survey aimed to:

    (a) determine the level of students' satisfaction with the attributes of the current program;

    (b) establish which attributes within each dimension were ranked by the students as most important to the success of their program;

    (c) determine if any of the attributes were perceived by the students as most important across all dimensions;

    (d) determine if other attributes, currently not included in the model, were identified by the students as critical to the effectiveness of the program.

The survey was divided into two sections; Section A aimed to determine the current status of the transnational program as perceived by the students, that is, measure the level of students' satisfaction with the various attributes of the program; Section B aimed to assess how students rank the attributes with respect to their perceived importance to the effectiveness of the program. A copy of the survey is included in Appendix A.

4.4.1. Satisfaction with the current transnational programs

Section A of the survey included a list of program attributes grouped in three broader categories: *Instruction/Instructor*, *Technology*, and *Program management and coordination*. Students were asked to evaluate each of the attributes using a five-point Likert scale, where 1 indicated *very poor*, 2 – *poor*, 3 – *average*, 4 – *good*, and 5 indicated *very good*. Data collected in this part of the survey was used to test the following hypotheses (referred to as hypotheses (5) through to (7) in Chapter 1, Section 1.2):

5. For each of the targeted programs, there will be no significant difference in the level of student satisfaction with the University instructor and the local instructor.

6. There will be no significant difference in the level of student satisfaction with transnational programs offered by the same University.

7. There will be no significant difference in the level of student satisfaction with transnational programs operated by the same offshore provider.

Sections 4.4.1.1 through 4.4.1.3 discuss the results of the survey used in the testing of these hypotheses. The summary of responses of the hypotheses' tests is presented in Section 4.4.1.4.

4.4.1.1. Satisfaction with Instruction/Instructor

The results related to students' satisfaction with attributes in the Instruction/Instruction category are reported in Table 4.4.1.1.a in two ways, firstly as percentages on the Likert scale (the percentages have been rounded to the nearest integer), and secondly as mean values.

Table 4.4.1.1.a. Satisfaction with *Instruction/Instructor*.

Attribute	Program1						Program2						Program3					
	Very poor (%)	Poor (%)	Avg (%)	Good (%)	Very good (%)	Mean	Very poor (%)	Poor (%)	Avg (%)	Good (%)	Very good (%)	Mean	Very poor (%)	Poor (%)	Avg (%)	Good (%)	Very good (%)	Mean
The clarity with which course objectives were communicated.	0	8	59	33	0	3.25	0	4	65	30	1	3.28	0	29	51	20	0	2.91
The time given in classes to copy down the presented lecture material.	4	6	55	33	2	3.23	2	14	58	26	0	3.10	4	20	56	20	0	2.91
The production quality of the lecture presentations.	0	6	48	40	6	3.46	0	17	55	28	0	3.11	2	36	60	2	0	2.62
The extent to which lecture presentations relied on electronic media.	2	6	34	50	8	3.56	1	7	56	34	2	3.27	2	13	54	29	2	3.16
The degree to which lecture notes and presentations helped you better understand the course material.	0	12	44	40	4	3.37	0	11	55	32	2	3.26	7	29	49	15	0	2.73
The time within which tests and written assignments were marked and returned.	4	21	56	15	4	2.94	15	32	38	12	3	2.55	42	38	20	0	0	1.78
The extent to which electronic media were used for assignment submission and feedback.	2	14	59	21	4	3.12	9	33	40	17	1	2.70	24	27	45	4	0	2.29
The degree to which instructional techniques that were used to teach the classes (e.g. demonstrations, group discussions, case studies, etc.) helped you better understand the course material.	0	4	56	38	2	3.38	0	21	55	24	0	3.01	4	42	45	9	0	2.58
The extent to which classrooms were free of distractions (e.g., noise from adjacent rooms, people coming in and out, other students talking with each other, etc.)	2	10	48	36	4	3.31	7	29	39	24	1	2.84	18	20	49	13	0	2.58
The extent to which instructors made the students feel that they were part of the class.	0	10	38	52	0	3.42	2	15	64	19	0	2.99	2	40	47	11	0	2.67
The instructors' communication skills.	0	8	29	54	9	3.65	1	13	56	30	0	3.16	2	31	60	7	0	2.71
The University instructors' organisation and preparation for classes.	2	6	48	38	6	3.40	0	8	47	41	4	3.42	0	31	56	13	0	2.82

☐ Attribute with highest level of satisfaction.

▨ Attribute with lowest level of satisfaction.

(Table 4.4.1.1.a continues over the page.)

(Table 4.4.1.a continued)

Attribute	Program1						Program2						Program3					
	Very poor (%)	Poor (%)	Avg (%)	Good (%)	Very good (%)	Mean	Very poor (%)	Poor (%)	Avg (%)	Good (%)	Very good (%)	Mean	Very poor (%)	Poor (%)	Avg (%)	Good (%)	Very good (%)	Mean
The Hong Kong instructors' organisation and preparation for classes.	2	0	46	35	17	3.65	2	19	49	28	2	3.11	11	33	51	5	0	2.49
The University instructors' dedication to students and teaching.	0	4	54	38	4	3.42	0	6	55	38	1	3.33	2	27	58	13	0	2.82
The Hong Kong instructors' dedication to students and teaching.	2	2	38	44	14	3.65	2	17	57	23	1	3.03	11	22	63	4	0	2.60
The University instructors' teaching ability.	0	4	61	31	4	3.35	0	6	46	44	4	3.46	0	18	73	9	0	2.91
The Hong Kong instructors' teaching ability.	0	4	46	40	10	3.56	2	12	55	29	2	3.17	9	24	65	2	0	2.60
The extent to which the University instructors encouraged class participation.	0	6	57	33	4	3.35	1	10	57	31	1	3.20	2	27	60	11	0	2.80
The extent to which the Hong Kong instructors encouraged class participation.	0	2	59	31	8	3.44	3	15	61	20	1	3.01	18	27	46	9	0	2.47
The telephone/email accessibility of the University instructors outside of classes.	0	15	54	29	2	3.17	7	24	51	16	2	2.84	20	22	40	18	0	2.56
The telephone/email accessibility of the Hong Kong instructors outside of classes.	0	10	42	44	4	3.42	9	22	50	17	2	2.81	18	20	38	24	0	2.69
The degree to which instructors encouraged communication between students, and between students and instructors.	2	8	52	36	2	3.29	1	21	62	15	1	2.94	16	22	51	11	0	2.58
The extent to which the course material was sufficient to support study at home (independent of class).	0	15	50	35	0	3.19	5	22	54	18	1	2.88	7	33	38	22	0	2.76
Overall, the University instructors were:	0	2	56	38	4	3.44	1	6	49	42	2	3.39	2	20	56	20	2	3.00
Overall, the Hong Kong instructors were:	0	6	44	39	11	3.56	3	17	52	28	0	3.06	13	27	53	7	0	2.53

Attribute with highest level of satisfaction.

Attribute with lowest level of satisfaction.

Program1

Students in Program1 were most satisfied with three attributes in the Instructor/Instruction category, namely: the communication skills of all the instructors, and two other attributes of the Hong Kong instructors, their organisation and preparation for classes, and dedication to students and teaching. All three attributes rated equally well (M=3.65), although there were some differences in response allocation, as illustrated in Table 4.4.1.1.b; results are reported as percentages on the Likert scale (the percentages have been rounded to the nearest integer), and mean values.

Table 4.4.1.1.b. Program1: highest ranking attributes in the *Instructor/Instruction* category.

Attribute	Very poor (%)	Poor (%)	Avg (%)	Good (%)	Very good (%)	Mean
The instructors' communication skills.	0	8	29	54	9	3.65
The Hong Kong instructors' dedication to students and teaching.	2	2	38	44	14	3.65
The Hong Kong instructors' organisation and preparation for classes.	2	0	46	35	17	3.65

While among the three highest rated attributes students' satisfaction with the communication skills of all the instructors attracted the highest number of 'Good' and 'Very good' responses (a total of 63%), it also scored the highest number of 'Poor' responses (8%). Hong Kong instructors' dedication to students and teaching was regarded by a smaller number of respondents as 'Very Poor' or 'Poor' (4%) but, at the same time, a smaller number of respondents rated it as 'Good' or 'Very good' (58%). Lastly, Hong Kong instructors' organisation and preparedness for classes, attracted the smallest number of negative responses (only 2%), and the smallest number of 'Good' and 'Very good' responses (a total of 52%); out of the three attributes, this attribute attracted the highest percentage of 'Average' responses (46%).

Students were least satisfied with the time taken by the instructors to mark and return written assignments and tests; 25% of students rated it 'Very poor' and 'Poor', while less than 20% considered it 'Good' or 'Very good'. Table 4.4.1.1.c presents the best and worst rated attributes, together with mean values and the percentage of all negative ('Very poor' and 'Poor' combined) and positive ('Good' and 'Very good' combined) responses for each of them.

Table 4.4.1.1.c. Program1: best and worst attributes in the *Instructor/Instruction* category in terms of student satisfaction.

	Attribute	Negative %	Positive %	Mean
Best	The instructors' communication skills.	8	63	3.65
	The Hong Kong instructors' dedication to students and teaching.	4	58	3.65
	The Hong Kong instructors' organisation and preparation for classes.	2	52	3.65
Worst	The time within which tests and written assignments were marked and returned.	25	19	2.94

Only nine out of twenty five attributes in the *Instructor/Instruction* category received any 'Very poor' responses and, even in those cases, the percentages of dissatisfied students were marginal (2% in seven attributes, 4% in each of the remaining two).

In addition, a comparison of student satisfaction with the University instructors and the Hong Kong instructors was performed to establish the presence of any significant differences. Although there was no significant difference in the overall level of student satisfaction with the University and Hong Kong instructors (Wilcoxon test; p=0.235), significant differences were discovered with respect to some individual attributes; in all those instances, students were more satisfied with the Hong Kong instructors. Students were significantly more satisfied with the Hong Kong instructors with respect to: the telephone/email accessibility outside of classes (Wilcoxon test; p=0.007); the organisation and preparedness for classes (Wilcoxon test; p=0.021); and dedication to students and teaching (Wilcoxon test; p=0.037). There was no significant difference in the satisfaction with the instructors' teaching ability (Wilcoxon test; p=0.051), and the extent to which instructors encouraged class participation (Wilcoxon test; p=0.358). The results of the comparisons together with the results of the Wilcoxon test are presented in Table 4.4.1.1.d.

Table 4.4.1.1.d. Program1: comparison of student satisfaction with University and
Hong Kong instructors.

Attribute	More satisfied with instructors from	Asymptotic significance (2-tailed)
Instructors' organisation and preparation for classes.	Hong Kong	p=0.021
Instructors' dedication to students and teaching.	Hong Kong	p=0.037
Instructors' teaching ability.	Hong Kong	p=0.051
The extent to which instructors encouraged class participation.	Hong Kong	p=0.358
The telephone/email accessibility of the instructors outside of classes.	Hong Kong	p=0.007
Overall satisfaction with instructors.	Hong Kong	p=0.235

The shading indicates a significantly greater level of satisfaction (p<0.05).

Program2

Students in this program were most satisfied with the attributes relating to University instructors; the instructors' teaching ability was rated highest, followed by the instructors' organisation and preparation for classes, and students' overall satisfaction with instructors. Students rated the University instructors' teaching ability highest (no 'Very poor' responses, and almost 50% of 'Good' and 'Very good' responses); similarly, the instructors' organisation and preparation for classes recorded no 'Very poor' scores and 45% of 'Very good'/'Good' responses; students' overall satisfaction with University instructors was rated similarly.

Students were least satisfied with the time taken by the instructors to mark and return written assignments and tests; almost 50% of the students were dissatisfied with it (15% rated it 'Very poor' and 32% rated it 'Poor'), while only 15% considered it 'Good'/'Very good'. Students were almost as dissatisfied with the extent to which electronic media were used for assignment submission and feedback (42% of 'Very poor'/'Poor' responses). A summary of best and worst rated attributes together with mean values and the percentage of negative and positive responses is presented in Table 4.4.1.1.e.

Table 4.4.1.1.e. Program2: best and worst attributes in the *Instructor/Instruction* category in terms of student satisfaction.

	Attribute	Negative %	Positive %	Mean
Best	The University instructors' teaching ability.	6	48	3.46
	The University instructors' organisation and preparation for classes.	8	45	3.42
	Overall satisfaction with University instructors.	7	44	3.39
Worst	The time within which tests and written assignments were marked and returned.	47	15	2.55
	The extent to which electronic media were used for assignment submission and feedback.	42	18	2.70

Eighteen out of twenty five attributes evaluated in this category received 'Very poor' responses; while in thirteen of those attributes the percentages of dissatisfied students were marginal and varied between 1% and 3%, the proportion of very dissatisfied students in the remaining five instances varied between 5% and 15%.

The comparison of student satisfaction with the University instructors and the Hong Kong instructors revealed that students were significantly more satisfied with the University instructors with respect to all but one attribute. Students were more satisfied with the University instructors' organisation and preparation for classes (Wilcoxon test; $p<0.001$); dedication to students and teaching (Wilcoxon test; $p<0.001$); teaching ability (Wilcoxon test; $p<0.001$); encouragement of class participation (Wilcoxon test; $p=0.002$); and, overall satisfaction with the instructors (Wilcoxon test; $p<0.001$). The only exception was the telephone/email accessibility of the instructors outside class; students were more satisfied with the Hong Kong instructors, but the difference was not significant (Wilcoxon test; $p=0.645$). The results of the comparisons together with the results of the Wilcoxon test are presented in Table 4.4.1.1.f.

Table 4.4.1.1.f. Program2: comparison of student satisfaction with University and Hong Kong instructors.

Attribute	More satisfied with instructors from	Asymptotic significance (2-tailed)
Instructors' organisation and preparation for classes.	University	$p < 0.001$
Instructors' dedication to students and teaching.	University	$p < 0.001$
Instructors' teaching ability.	University	$p < 0.001$
The extent to which instructors encouraged class participation.	University	$p = 0.002$
The telephone/email accessibility of the instructors outside of classes.	Hong Kong	$p = 0.645$
Overall satisfaction with instructors.	University	$p < 0.001$

☐ The shading indicates a significantly greater level of satisfaction ($p < 0.05$).

Program3

Students in this program were most satisfied with the extent to which lecture presentations relied on electronic media (29% of 'Good' responses, and 2% of 'Very good' responses). Overall performance of University instructors was the second attribute with which students were most satisfied (20% of 'Good' and 2% of 'Very good' responses). These were the only two attributes, out of a total of twenty-five in the Instructor/Instruction category, for which 'Very good' responses were recorded.

The level of student satisfaction, or rather dissatisfaction, with the time taken by the instructors to mark and return written assignments and tests was very high; 80% of the students were dissatisfied with it (42% rated it 'Very poor' and 38% rated it 'Poor'), while the remaining 20% rated it average; there were no 'Good' or 'Very good' responses. A summary of negative and positive responses for the best and worst rated attributes is presented in Table 4.4.1.1.g.

Table 4.4.1.1.g. Program3: best and worst attributes in the *Instructor/Instruction* category in terms of student satisfaction.

	Attribute	Negative %	Positive %	Mean
Best	The extent to which lecture presentations relied on electronic media.	15	31	3.16
	Overall satisfaction with University instructors.	22	22	3.00
Worst	The time within which tests and written assignments were marked and returned.	80	0	1.78

An overwhelming twenty two out of twenty five attributes in this category received 'Very poor' responses; while nine of those attributes recorded relatively small percentages of dissatisfied students, varying between 2% and 4%, the proportion of students very dissatisfied with the remaining thirteen attributes ranged between 7% and 42%.

The comparison of student satisfaction with the University instructors and the Hong Kong instructors revealed that, overall, students were significantly more satisfied with the University than with the Hong Kong instructors. Students were more satisfied with University instructors with respect to their: organisation and preparation for classes (Wilcoxon test; p=0.029); teaching ability (Wilcoxon test; p=0.019); encouragement of class participation (Wilcoxon test; p=0.027); and, overall satisfaction with the instructors (Wilcoxon test; p=0.007). The only exceptions were: instructors' dedication to students and teaching – University instructors were preferred, but the difference was not significant (Wilcoxon test; p=0.09); and, telephone/email accessibility of the instructors outside class – students were more satisfied with the Hong Kong instructors, but the difference was not significant (Wilcoxon test; p=0.366). A summary of the comparisons together with the results of the Wilcoxon test is presented in Table 4.4.1.1.h.

Table 4.4.1.1.h. Program3: comparison of student satisfaction with University and Hong Kong instructors.

Attribute	More satisfied with instructors from	Asymptotic significance (2-tailed)
Instructors' organisation and preparation for classes.	University	p=0.029
Instructors' dedication to students and teaching.	University	p=0.090
Instructors' teaching ability.	University	p=0.019
The extent to which instructors encouraged class participation.	University	p=0.027
The telephone/email accessibility of the instructors outside of classes.	Hong Kong	p=0.366
Overall satisfaction with instructors.	University	p=0.007

☐   The shading indicates a significantly greater level of satisfaction (p<0.05).

4.4.1.2. Satisfaction with Technology

The results related to students' satisfaction with attributes in the *Technology* cluster are reported in Table 4.4.1.2.a as percentages on the Likert scale and as mean values; percentages have been rounded to the nearest integer.

Table 4.4.1.2.a. Satisfaction with *Technology*.

Attribute	Program1						Program2						Program3					
	Very poor (%)	Poor (%)	Avg (%)	Good (%)	Very good (%)	Mean	Very poor (%)	Poor (%)	Avg (%)	Good (%)	Very good (%)	Mean	Very poor (%)	Poor (%)	Avg (%)	Good (%)	Very good (%)	Mean
The quality of the technology used in classes.	0	12	38	42	8	3.46	4	23	57	15	1	2.86	11	27	49	13	0	2.64
The ease of use of technology.	0	6	40	46	8	3.56	2	16	66	15	1	2.98	9	20	51	20	0	2.82
The extent to which the course relied on the use of technology in the classroom or the college.	0	8	42	46	4	3.46	2	19	65	14	0	2.91	11	29	42	16	2	2.69
The extent to which the course relied on the use of technology at home.	0	4	69	25	2	3.25	3	22	56	19	0	2.93	2	22	69	7	0	2.80
The degree of confidence you had that classes would not be interrupted or cancelled due to technical problems.	0	2	60	34	4	3.40	1	15	58	25	1	3.11	11	27	44	18	0	2.69
The quality of technical support provided.	0	6	50	40	4	3.42	6	24	59	11	0	2.76	20	18	44	18	0	2.60
The overall usefulness of course Web sites.	2	6	40	48	4	3.46	5	16	54	24	1	3.00	11	24	36	29	0	2.82

Attribute with highest level of satisfaction.

Attribute with lowest level of satisfaction.

Program1

Student satisfaction with the attributes of the *Technology* category was similar across all attributes. While the ease of use of technology was regarded highest – it received 54% of favourable responses (46% 'Good' and 8% 'Very good') and only 6% of 'Poor' ones – the extent to which the course relied on the use of technology at home rated lowest with 27% of favourable responses (25% 'Good' and 2% 'Very good') and 4% of 'Poor' responses. A summary of favourable and negative responses for the best and worst rated attributes in the Technology category is presented in Table 4.4.1.2.b.

Table 4.4.1.2.b. Program1: best and worst attributes in the *Technology* category in terms of student satisfaction.

	Attribute	Negative %	Positive %	Mean
Best	The ease of use of technology.	6	54	3.56
Worst	The extent to which the course relied on the use of technology at home.	4	27	3.25

The percentage of favourable responses for the remaining attributes in this category varied between 44% and 52%. Only one attribute in this category, the overall usefulness of the subject Web sites, received a 'Very poor' response, but it was a marginal 2%.

Program2

Students in this program were most satisfied with the fact that classes were unlikely to be cancelled or interrupted due to technical problems (26% of favourable responses; 1% 'Very Poor' and 15% 'Poor' responses). Students reported lowest satisfaction with the quality of the provided technical support (only 11% of 'Good' responses and 30% of negative ones). A summary of favourable and negative responses for the best and worst rated attributes in this category is presented in Table 4.4.1.2.c.

Table 4.4.1.2.c. Program2: best and worst attributes in the *Technology* category in terms of student satisfaction.

	Attribute	Negative %	Positive %	Mean
Best	The degree of confidence you had that classes would not be interrupted or cancelled due to technical problems.	16	26	3.11
Worst	The quality of technical support provided.	30	11	2.76

The reported level of satisfaction across the remaining attributes in this category was similar and varied between 18% and 27% on the negative side, and 14% and 25% on the positive side. 'Very poor' responses were recorded for all attributes in this category and the percentage of those responses ranged from 1% to 6%. 'Very good' responses were recorded for only four out of seven attributes in this category and their percentage was a minimal 1% in all instances.

Program3

Student satisfaction with the *Technology* attributes in this program was low. Students were relatively most satisfied with the ease of use of technology (20% of 'Good' responses and nearly 30% of negative responses), and the overall usefulness of the course Web sites (nearly 30% of 'Good' responses and 35% of negative responses). Students were least satisfied with the quality of the provided technical support (18% of 'Good' responses and 20% of 'Very Poor' and 18% of 'Poor' responses). A summary of positive and negative responses for the best and worst rated attributes in this category is presented in Table 4.4.1.2.d.

Table 4.4.1.2.d. Program3: best and worst attributes in the *Technology* category in terms of student satisfaction.

	Attribute	Negative %	Positive %	Mean
Best	The ease of use of technology.	29	20	2.82
	The overall usefulness of the course Web sites.	35	29	2.82
Worst	The quality of technical support provided.	38	18	2.60

Only one attribute – the extent to which the course relied on the use of technology in the classroom or the college – received a 'Very good' response, but it was a marginal 2%. 'Very poor' responses were recorded for all attributes; the percentage for one of them – the reliance of the use of technology at home – was a marginal 2%; the largest 'Very Poor' percentage was that of 20% for 'the quality of technical support provided'; and, the remaining attributes averaged an 11%.

4.4.1.3. Satisfaction with Course Management and Coordination

The results related to students' satisfaction with attributes in the *Course management and coordination* cluster are reported in Table 4.4.1.3.a as percentages on the Likert scale and mean values; percentages have been rounded to the nearest integer.

Table 4.4.1.3.a. Satisfaction with *Course management and coordination*.

Attribute	Program1						Program2						Program3					
	Very poor (%)	Poor (%)	Avg (%)	Good (%)	Very good (%)	Mean	Very poor (%)	Poor (%)	Avg (%)	Good (%)	Very good (%)	Mean	Very poor (%)	Poor (%)	Avg (%)	Good (%)	Very good (%)	Mean
The present means of exchanging course material between you and the instructors.	0	15	60	23	2	3.12	1	24	63	12	0	2.85	7	33	56	4	0	2.58
Your ability to access the university library and other student resources.	10	23	55	10	2	2.71	10	35	43	12	0	2.57	27	40	24	9	0	2.16
Your ability to access a computer when, and if, needed.	2	13	54	29	2	3.15	6	22	50	21	1	2.90	20	29	33	16	2	2.51
The general attitude of the administrative/technical staff, e.g. in delivering materials, maintaining classrooms.	0	4	56	38	2	3.38	9	18	56	17	0	2.82	25	33	29	13	0	2.31
The accessibility of administrative/technical staff.	0	6	44	48	2	3.46	6	23	55	16	0	2.82	22	20	49	9	0	2.44
The promptness with which course materials were delivered.	2	6	54	36	2	3.31	3	23	56	18	0	2.89	18	29	46	7	0	2.42
Your ability to access the university course coordinator when needed.	0	12	42	44	2	3.37	3	25	58	13	1	2.84	16	33	44	7	0	2.42
Class enrollment and registration procedures.	2	4	48	42	4	3.42	8	29	42	20	1	2.77	15	38	40	7	0	2.38
Your opportunity to evaluate the course.	0	6	52	38	4	3.40	3	16	59	21	1	3.02	18	44	36	2	0	2.22
The extent to which, in your opinion, the university responds to evaluations.	0	10	52	34	4	3.33	4	19	66	11	0	2.85	32	20	41	7	0	2.24
The degree of organisational support.	2	2	58	34	4	3.37	3	20	65	12	0	2.86	22	38	36	4	0	2.24

☐ Attribute with highest level of satisfaction.

▨ Attribute with lowest level of satisfaction.

Program1

In the category of *Course management and coordination* students were most satisfied with the accessibility of administrative and technical staff (48% of 'Good' and 2% of 'Very good' responses, and only 6% of 'Poor' ones). Student satisfaction with enrollment and registration procedures was almost equally high (46% of positive and 6% of negative responses). Students were least satisfied with two aspects of this category: their ability to access the university library and other student resources (33% of students rated this attribute as unsatisfactory, and 12% as satisfactory); and, the present means of exchanging course materials between students and instructors (15% of negative and 25% of positive responses). A summary of positive and negative responses for the best and worst rated attributes in this category is presented in Table 4.4.1.3.b.

Table 4.4.1.3.b. Program1: best and worst attributes in the *Course management and coordination* category in terms of student satisfaction.

	Attribute	Negative %	Positive %	Mean
Best	The accessibility of administrative/technical staff.	6	50	3.46
	Class enrollment and registration procedures.	6	46	3.42
Worst	The ability to access the university library and other student resources.	33	12	2.71
	The present means of exchanging course materials between you and the instructors.	15	25	3.12

The percentages of favourable responses for the remaining attributes in this category varied between 31% and 46%, while the percentages of negative responses ranged from 4% to 15%.

Program2

Students in this program were most satisfied with the opportunity to evaluate it (22% of positive responses and 19% of negative responses). They were least satisfied with two aspects of *Course management and coordination*: access to the university library and other student resources (45% of negative responses and 12% of positive responses); and, class enrollment and registration procedures (37% of negative and 21% of positive responses). The satisfaction with other attributes in this category ranged from 12% to 22% on the positive side, and 21% to 29% on the negative side. Table 4.4.1.3.c presents a summary positive and negative responses for the best and worst rated attributes in the *Course management and coordination* category.

96

Table 4.4.1.3.c. Program2: best and worst attributes in the *Course management and coordination* category in terms of student satisfaction.

	Attribute	Negative %	Positive %	Mean
Best	Your opportunity to evaluate the course.	19	21	3.02
Worst	The ability to access the university library and other student resources.	45	12	2.57
	Class enrolment and registration procedures.	37	21	2.77

Program3

Student satisfaction with the attributes of the *Course management and coordination* in this program was low. Students were relatively most satisfied with the present means of exchanging course material (4% of 'Good' and 40% of 'Very Poor' and 'Poor' responses), and their ability to access a computer when, and if, needed (18% of 'Good' and 'Very good' responses, and 49% of 'Very Poor' and 'Poor' responses). Students were decidedly most dissatisfied with their ability to access the university library with nearly 70% of students rating it negatively (27% of 'Very Poor' and 40% of 'Poor' responses). The percentages of negative responses for all the remaining attributes of this category ranged between 39% and 62%. Only one attribute – ability to access a computer when, and if, needed – recorded a marginal 2% 'Very Good' response but it also attracted 49% of negative responses. Table 4.4.1.3.d presents a summary of positive and negative responses for the best and worst rated attributes in the *Course management and coordination* category.

Table 4.4.1.3.d. Program3: best and worst attributes in the *Course management and coordination* category in terms of student satisfaction.

	Attribute	Negative %	Positive %	Mean
Best	The present means of exchanging course material between you and instructors.	40	4	2.58
	Your ability to access a computer when, and if, needed.	49	18	2.51
Worst	The ability to access the university library and other student resources.	67	9	2.16

4.4.1.4. Summary of responses to hypotheses (5) – (7)

Part A of the survey was used to test hypotheses regarding student satisfaction with the current transnational computing programs. The data for hypotheses (5) through (7) was collected from students participating in the evaluated programs, and a summary of results was presented in Sections 4.4.1.1 through to 4.4.1.3. This section provides a summary of responses to the abovementioned hypotheses.

Hypothesis (5):

For each of the targeted programs, there will be no significant difference in the level of student satisfaction with the University instructor and the local instructor.

To test this hypothesis, data was analysed on survey items pertaining to University and local (Hong Kong) instructors: organisation and preparation for classes, dedication to students and teaching, teaching ability, encouragement of class participation, telephone/email accessibility outside of classes, and overall satisfaction with the instructors.

This hypothesis was not supported; findings in two out of three evaluated programs did not support the hypothesis. Students in Program2 and Program3 reported a significantly higher level of overall satisfaction with the University instructors (Wilcoxon test; $p < 0.001$ and $p = 0.007$ respectively). They were also significantly more satisfied with most individual aspects of University instructors' performance; the only aspect where the level of satisfaction was higher, but not significantly, with the Hong Kong instructors was accessibility outside of classes. Students in Program1 were more satisfied with local instructors with respect to both their overall performance and all of its individual aspects; the difference in overall level of satisfaction with Hong Kong instructors as compared to University instructors was not significant (Wilcoxon test; $p = 0.235$). A summary of findings relating to the outcome of hypothesis (5) is presented in Table 4.4.1.4.

Table 4.4.1.4. Student satisfaction with University and Hong Kong instructors.
(Including preferred instructors and significance of preference.)

Aspect	Program 1	Program 2	Program 3
Organisation and preparation for classes.	Hong Kong, $p=0.021$	University, $p<0.001$	University, $p=0.029$
Dedication to students and teaching.	Hong Kong, $p=0.037$	University, $p<0.001$	University, $p=0.090$
Teaching ability.	Hong Kong, $p=0.051$	University, $p<0.001$	University, $p=0.019$
Encouragement of class participation.	Hong Kong, $p=0.358$	University, $p=0.002$	University, $p=0.027$
Telephone/email accessibility outside of classes.	Hong Kong, $p=0.007$	Hong Kong, $p=0.645$	Hong Kong, $p=0.366$
Overall satisfaction.	Hong Kong, $p=0.235$	University, $p<0.001$	University, $p=0.007$

The shading indicates a significantly greater level of satisfaction ($p<0.05$).

Hypothesis (6):

There will be no significant difference in the level of student satisfaction with transnational programs offered by the same University.

To test this hypothesis, data was analysed on survey items which included all the attributes in categories *Instructor/Instruction*, *Technology*, and *Course management and coordination*. The analysis included only data for programs Program1 and Program2, as they were offered by the same University – University A.

This hypothesis was not supported. An independent-samples t-test was conducted to compare the average student satisfaction scores. There was a significant difference in scores for students in Program1 (M=3.36, SD=0.43), and Program2 (M=2.99, SD=0.38); t=5.96, p<0.001.

Hypothesis (7):

There will be no significant difference in the level of student satisfaction with transnational programs operated by the same offshore provider.

To test this hypothesis, data was analysed on survey items including all the attributes in categories *Instructor/Instruction*, *Technology*, and *Course management and coordination*; the analysis included only data for programs Program2 and Program3, as they were operated by the same offshore provider – the same partner institution in Hong Kong – Partner B.

This hypothesis was not supported. An independent-samples t-test was conducted to compare the average student satisfaction scores. There was a significant difference in scores for students in Program2 (M=2.99, SD=0.38), and Program3 (M=2.59, SD=0.46); t=5.92, p<0.001.

4.4.2. Perceived effectiveness of the current transnational education programs – Response to hypothesis (8)

The survey also sought students' perceptions regarding the effectiveness of the transnational programs in which they currently participated (Appendix A; Survey section A, questions 38 and 39). The perceptions varied across the three evaluated programs. While students in Program1 and Program2 by and large perceived their programs as effective (85% and 78% respectively), perceptions of students in Program3 were polarised – 49% of students found the program effective, whereas 51% of them disagreed.

Students were asked to justify their opinions. Those who regarded their programs as effective cited various reasons for program effectiveness including: the opportunity to obtain a University degree while working full time; flexible program structure; good quality of study material provided by the University; and promising job prospects upon completion of the program. Students who did not regard their programs as effective blamed it on: poor attitude and poor teaching skills of local instructors; lack of feedback on assessment tasks; poor administrative services; excessive emphasis on self-study; overload of study material and hasty pace of study; and, inadequate technological support for a degree program.

The effectiveness of current programs was also gauged in a different way; namely, students were asked if they would participate in this type of program, that is a transnational program, in the future. Here, the results for all three programs were less favourable than those obtained through gathering students' perceptions about the current programs. While in Program1 the percentage of students dropped to 69% (from the previous 85%); the biggest drop was recorded for students in Program2, from 78% to 47%. Students in Program3 were consistent in their perception of program effectiveness with a drop of only 2% from the original 49%. A summary of the perceived effectiveness of the current programs is presented in Table 4.4.2.

Table 4.4.2. Perceived effectiveness of current programs – percentage of students.

	Program1		Program2		Program3	
	Yes	No	Yes	No	Yes	No
Is the current program effective?	85	15	78	22	49	51
Would you participate in this type of program in the future?	69	31	47	53	47	53

Hypothesis (8):

Each of the targeted transnational programs will be perceived by its students as effective.

This hypothesis was not supported as not all of the targeted programs were perceived by their students as effective. The hypothesis was only fully supported with respect to Program1 as students in this program considered it effective and were also willing to participate in this type of program in the future. The hypothesis was only partly supported for Program2 – students considered the program effective, however the majority would not enroll in a similar type of program in the future. There was no support for the hypothesis in Program3.

4.4.3. Relative importance of program attributes within dimensions

Section B of the survey included program attributes grouped in ten dimensions: *Student, University instructor and learning environment, Hong Kong instructor and learning environment, University instructor – Technology and organisation; Hong Kong instructor – Technology and organisation, Curriculum and instruction design, Interaction, Evaluation and assessment, Technology,* and *Program management and organisational support.* In each dimension, students ranked only the top three attributes that they considered most important to the effectiveness of the program, where first indicated *most important*, second – *important*, and third – *somewhat important*; students left the remaining attributes in the dimension without a rank thus considering those *not important.*

Data collected in this part of the survey was used to test hypotheses (1) through (4):
1. Critical success attributes (of effective distance education programs) in each dimension will be evident in each targeted transnational program.
2. Some attributes will be regarded as more important to the success of transnational programs than others.
3. Additional attributes, not included in the current dimensional model, will be identified as critical to the effectiveness of transnational programs.
4. In each of the targeted programs, attributes regarded as important with respect to University instructor, will be also regarded as important with respect to local instructor.

The conclusions of the hypotheses' tests are presented in Section 4.4.3.12.

To enable simple, that is based on a single value, ranking of attributes within a dimension, the first, second, and third preferences were weighted as follows: first preference was assigned a weight of 3, second preference – 2, third preference – 1, and lack of preference – 0. Thus the weighted sum of an attribute which, for instance, attracted 14 first preferences, 4 second preferences, and 2 third preferences would equal 52 as a result of the following calculation:

$$(14*3) + (4*2) + (2*1) = 42 + 8 + 2 = 52$$

The overall importance of an attribute within a dimension was obtained from the sum of the weighted student preferences for that dimension.

The ranking results for attributes in each dimension are presented in two ways; firstly, as percentages of students that ranked each attribute first, second, and third in terms of their importance to the effectiveness of the program; and, secondly, as weighted sums of student preferences for each attribute.

4.4.3.1. Ranking of attributes in the dimension *Student*

First, students ranked the attributes in the dimension *Student* in terms of their importance to the effectiveness of transnational computing education programs. The ranking of attributes in this dimension is presented in Table 4.4.3.1. For clarity of presentation, percentages have been rounded to the nearest integer.

Table 4.4.3.1. Dimension *Student*: ranking of attributes.

Attribute	Program1 (N=48)					Program2 (N=160)					Program3 (N=45)				
	1st (%)	2nd (%)	3rd (%)	None (%)	Weighted sum	1st (%)	2nd (%)	3rd (%)	None (%)	Weighted sum	1st (%)	2nd (%)	3rd (%)	None (%)	Weighted sum
Works as a team player	29	8	4	59	52	13	14	10	63	120	13	16	4	67	34
Has positive attitude towards technology-based learning	19	15	17	49	49	29	18	11	42	215	27	13	18	42	56
Is motivated and self-disciplined	25	25	23	27	71	28	23	16	33	231	20	20	16	44	52
Is confident in using technology	6	10	21	63	29	11	17	21	51	138	4	9	18	69	22
Knows how to work independently	8	13	13	66	30	11	15	18	56	131	18	20	7	55	45
Is involved and participates	6	17	8	69	29	6	8	14	72	75	9	13	13	65	30
Is willing to ask instructors for assistance	6	13	15	66	28	3	6	11	80	50	9	9	27	55	32

The most important attribute in the dimension.

Second most important attribute in the dimension.

Third most important attribute in the dimension.

According to the weighted sums, students in Program1 ranked *'Is motivated and self-disciplined'*, *'Works as a team player'*, and *'Has positive attitude towards technology-based learning'* as the three most important attributes of the Student dimension. Although *'Works as a team player'* received the highest percentage, 29%, of first preferences out of the three highest ranked attributes, it received only 8% and 4% of second and third preferences respectively. In comparison, *'Is motivated and self-disciplined'*, received fewer first preferences, 25%, but a significantly greater number of second and third preferences, 25% and 23% respectively, and rated much better overall. The remaining four attributes in this dimension were perceived by students to have a much lesser impact on the effectiveness of the program than the top three attributes. The four attributes received almost identical scores, whereby the attribute *'Is willing to ask instructors for assistance'* was regarded as least important of the four by a very small margin.

While students in the second program, Program2, also ranked *'Is motivated and self-disciplined'* and *'Has positive attitude towards technology-based learning'* as first and second most influential attribute overall, they selected *'Is confident in using technology'* as the third most important attribute. Students in this program, like their counterparts in Program1, also ranked *'Is willing to ask instructors for assistance'* lowest, with 80% of students attaching no importance to the attribute.

Students in the third program, Program3, ranked *'Has positive attitude towards technology-based learning'* highest, both in terms of the number of first choices, 27%, as well as overall. *'Is motivated and self-disciplined'*, and *'Knows how to work independently'* were clearly ranked as second and third. Students nominated *'Is confident in using technology'* as an attribute of least impact on the effectiveness of the program.

4.4.3.2. Ranking of attributes in the dimension *University instructor and learning environment*

Next, students ranked the attributes in the *University instructor and learning environment* dimension in terms of their importance to the effectiveness of transnational computing education programs. The results, with percentages rounded to the nearest integer, are presented in Table 4.4.3.2.

Table 4.4.3.2. Dimension *University instructor and learning environment*: ranking of attributes.

Attribute	Program1 (N=48)					Program2 (N=160)					Program3 (N=45)				
	1st (%)	2nd (%)	3rd (%)	None (%)	Weighted sum	1st (%)	2nd (%)	3rd (%)	None (%)	Weighted sum	1st (%)	2nd (%)	3rd (%)	None (%)	Weighted sum
Understands course requirements, students' characteristics and needs.	48	19	2	31	88	37	18	17	28	262	31	20	13	36	66
Encourages students to take responsibility for their own learning.	8	15	6	71	29	9	11	10	70	97	4	2	4	90	10
Encourages communication between students, and students and instructors.	8	25	19	48	45	11	22	17	50	148	18	20	18	44	50
Demonstrates dedication to course, teaching and students.	13	6	15	66	31	11	16	13	60	124	9	9	13	69	26
Uses effective communication skills.	8	15	17	60	34	26	21	13	40	212	31	33	18	18	80
Conducts students' needs assessment and course evaluation.	13	13	17	57	38	4	5	16	75	59	4	13	22	61	28
Ensures students' support services.	2	8	25	65	23	3	7	15	75	58	2	2	11	85	10

The most important attribute in the dimension.

Second most important attribute in the dimension.

Third most important attribute in the dimension.

Students in Program1 gave a clear highest ranking in this dimension to the attribute *'Understands course requirements, students' characteristics and needs'*, with 67% of the students making it their first or second choice. *'Encourages communication between students, and students and instructors'* was rated second with a combined total of 33% of first and second choices, followed by *'Conducts students' needs assessment and course evaluation'*.

Like their counterparts in Program1, students in Program2 also rated *'Understands course requirements, students' characteristics and needs'* highest, with 55% of students making it their first or second choice. *'Uses effective communication skills'* was rated as second in terms of overall importance (47% of first and second choices), while *'Encourages communication between students, and students and instructors'* was rated third.

Students in Program3 selected the same three most important attributes as students in Program2, albeit in a different order of importance; *'Uses effective communication skills'* was rated highest (64% of first and second preferences), followed by *'Understands course requirements, students' characteristics and needs'* and *'Encourages communication between students, and students and instructors'*.

'Ensures students' support services' was rated lowest in all three programs, with the percentage of students attaching no importance to this attribute ranging from 65% in Program1, to 75% in Program2, and 85% in Program3.

4.4.3.3. Ranking of attributes in the dimension *Hong Kong instructor and learning environment*

Next, students ranked attributes in the dimension *Hong Kong instructor and learning environment*. Results, with percentages rounded to the nearest integer, are presented in Table 4.4.3.3.

Table 4.4.3.3. Dimension *Hong Kong instructor and learning environment*: ranking of attributes.

Attribute	Program1 (N=48)					Program2 (N=160)					Program3 (N=45)				
	1st (%)	2nd (%)	3rd (%)	None (%)	Weighted sum	1st (%)	2nd (%)	3rd (%)	None (%)	Weighted sum	1st (%)	2nd (%)	3rd (%)	None (%)	Weighted sum
Understands course requirements, students' characteristics and needs.	46	4	13	37	76	37	16	16	31	254	31	24	9	36	68
Encourages students to take responsibility for their own learning.	8	25	10	57	41	11	11	13	65	109	9	4	4	83	18
Encourages communication between students, and students and instructors.	17	17	2	64	41	11	19	16	54	139	7	24	22	47	41
Demonstrates dedication to course, teaching and students.	8	15	21	56	36	9	18	19	54	131	13	9	11	67	31
Uses effective communication skills.	15	23	23	39	54	23	20	16	41	200	36	16	24	24	73
Conducts students' needs assessment and course evaluation.	4	13	8	75	22	2	10	11	77	58	4	11	20	65	25
Ensures students' support services.	2	4	23	71	18	6	7	11	76	69	2	11	9	78	17

The most important attribute in the dimension.

Second most important attribute in the dimension.

Third most important attribute in the dimension.

Students in Program1 gave the highest ranking in this dimension to the attribute *'Understands course requirements, students' characteristics and needs'*, with 46% of the students giving the attribute their first preference. Other attributes selected by the students as the most influential were *'Uses effective communication skills'* and *'Encourages students to take responsibility for their own learning'* (tied in second place), and *'Encourages communication between students, and students and instructors'*.

Students in Program2 ranked the three most important attributes in this dimension in a similar manner as students in Program1; the only difference was the absence of the attribute *'Encourages students to take responsibility for their own learning'* tied in the second place.

Students in Program3 selected the same three attributes as students in the other programs, albeit in a different order of importance; *'Uses effective communication skills'* was ranked highest, followed by *'Understands course requirements, students' characteristics and needs'* and *'Encourages communication between students, and students and instructors'*.

'Ensures students' support services' and *'Conducts students' needs assessment and course evaluation'* were the attributes ranked lowest in all three programs.

4.4.3.4. Ranking of attributes in the dimension *University instructor –*
Technology and organisation

The attributes in the dimension *University instructor – Technology and organisation* were ranked next; the ranking results, with percentages rounded to the nearest integer are presented in Table 4.4.3.4.

Table 4.4.3.4. Dimension *University instructor – Technology and organisation*: ranking of attributes.

Attribute	Program1 (N=48)					Program2 (N=160)					Program3 (N=45)				
	1st (%)	2nd (%)	3rd (%)	None (%)	Weighted sum	1st (%)	2nd (%)	3rd (%)	None (%)	Weighted sum	1st (%)	2nd (%)	3rd (%)	None (%)	Weighted sum
Has positive attitude towards technology.	15	8	10	67	34	14	8	12	66	109	0	4	13	83	10
Demonstrates control over technology.	6	13	6	75	24	7	7	5	81	63	2	4	16	78	14
Adapts course materials for delivery through electronic media.	8	6	13	73	24	6	11	11	72	78	9	7	22	62	28
Has experience with technology-based courses.	15	10	4	71	33	18	13	17	52	154	13	13	11	63	35
Is well prepared and organised.	33	29	6	32	79	38	18	11	33	256	27	22	9	42	60
Is proficient in instructional design.	10	8	17	65	31	3	14	9	74	70	13	18	2	67	35
Uses interactive instructional strategies.	4	8	10	78	19	4	9	13	74	69	0	11	13	76	16
Provides well-designed syllabus and presentation outlines.	8	17	19	56	37	11	21	18	50	146	36	13	13	38	66
Develops effective graphics.	0	0	15	85	7	1	1	5	93	15	0	7	0	93	6

The most important attribute in the dimension.

Second most important attribute in the dimension.

Third most important attribute in the dimension.

Students in Program1 singled out *'Is well prepared and organised'* as the attribute having most influence on this dimension; it received an overwhelming majority of 62% of first and second preferences. The two next most important dimensions, *'Provides well-designed syllabus and presentation outlines'* and *'Has positive attitude towards technology'*, trailed well behind the top one.

Students in Program2 selected the same most influential attribute as students from Program1, also giving the attribute a clear winning rank (56% of first and second preferences). *'Has experience with technology-based courses'* and *'Provides well-designed syllabus and presentation outlines'* were ranked second and third respectively.

Students in Program3 declared *'Provides well-designed syllabus and presentation outlines'* as the attribute of most importance. However, it was followed closely by the second most important attribute – *'Is well prepared and organised'*. The third place was a tie between *'Has experience with technology-based courses'* and *'Is proficient with instructional design'*.

The one attribute barely noticed by students in all three programs was *'Develops effective graphics'*. It received no first or second choices from students in Program1, and no first or third choices from students in Program3; the percentage of students who attached no importance to the attribute ranged from 85% in Program1, to 93% in each of Program2 and Program3.

4.4.3.5. Ranking of attributes in the dimension *Hong Kong instructor –*
Technology and organisation

Attributes in the dimension *Hong Kong instructor – Technology and organisation* were ranked next; the ranking results in this dimension, with percentages rounded to the nearest integer, are presented in Table 4.4.3.5.

Table 4.4.3.5. Dimension *Hong Kong instructor – Technology and organisation*: ranking of attributes.

Attribute	Program1 (N=49)					Program2 (N=160)					Program3 (N=45)				
	1st (%)	2nd (%)	3rd (%)	None (%)	Weighted sum	1st (%)	2nd (%)	3rd (%)	None (%)	Weighted sum	1st (%)	2nd (%)	3rd (%)	None (%)	Weighted sum
Has positive attitude towards technology.	12	8	6	74	29	13	8	14	65	106	4	9	18	69	22
Demonstrates control over technology.	6	6	18	70	24	6	7	8	79	62	7	9	13	71	23
Adapts course materials for delivery through electronic media.	10	16	12	62	37	11	10	13	66	103	9	11	16	64	29
Has experience with technology-based courses.	20	8	8	64	42	18	21	13	48	173	13	13	11	63	35
Is well prepared and organised.	39	16	18	27	82	36	14	13	37	237	33	29	9	29	75
Is proficient in instructional design.	4	10	10	76	21	3	13	7	77	65	7	9	4	80	19
Uses interactive instructional strategies.	2	22	8	68	29	5	11	13	71	81	2	9	22	67	21
Provides well-designed syllabus and presentation outlines.	6	12	8	74	25	9	14	15	62	115	24	7	7	62	42
Develops effective graphics.	0	0	10	90	5	1	2	6	91	18	0	4	0	96	4

The most important attribute in the dimension.

Second most important attribute in the dimension.

Third most important attribute in the dimension.

In this dimension, the attribute *'Is well prepared and organised'* was ranked as most important by students in all three programs receiving 55%, 50%, and 62% of first and second choices from students in the respective programs. In all programs, this attribute was rated highest with respect to the number of first choices, 39%, 36%, and 33% respectively, as well as overall.

Students in Program1 and Program2 ranked *'Has experience with technology-based courses'* second. Their third choices were *'Adapts course materials for delivery through electronic media'* in Program1, and *'Provides well-designed syllabus and presentation outlines'* in Program2.

Students in Program3 ranked *'Provides well-designed syllabus and presentation outlines'* second, and *'Has experience with technology-based courses'* third.

'Develops effective graphics' was ranked by students in all three programs as the attribute of least importance to this dimension; it was given no first or second choices by students in Program1, and no first or third choices by students in Program3; the percentage of students who attached no importance to the attribute ranged from 90% in Program1, to 91% in Program2, and 96% in Program3.

4.4.3.6. Ranking of attributes in the dimension *Curriculum and instruction design*

Next, the attributes in the dimension *Curriculum and instruction design* were ranked; the results are presented in Table 4.4.3.6. For clarity of presentation, percentages have been rounded to the nearest integer.

Table 4.4.3.6. Dimension *Curriculum and instruction design*: ranking of attributes.

Attribute	Program1 (N=49)					Program2 (N=160)					Program3 (N=45)				
	1st (%)	2nd (%)	3rd (%)	None (%)	Weighted sum	1st (%)	2nd (%)	3rd (%)	None (%)	Weighted sum	1st (%)	2nd (%)	3rd (%)	None (%)	Weighted sum
Relates the new material to previous student knowledge.	21	16	8	55	50	17	9	11	63	127	22	9	18	51	46
Integrates all course elements into a well-paced package.	25	8	6	61	47	18	15	12	55	151	13	9	9	69	30
Is relevant to job/career.	33	20	14	33	75	34	12	8	46	213	27	27	9	37	64
Creates logical sequences for each element presented.	8	12	22	58	35	8	19	13	60	117	11	11	11	67	30
Course objectives and learning outcomes are communicated to students.	8	16	8	68	32	14	23	23	40	176	13	22	20	45	47
Instructors and students agree on deadlines for completion and marking of assignments.	4	8	20	68	24	3	11	13	73	72	7	16	18	59	31
Learning objectives are supported by instructional methodologies.	2	18	20	60	31	8	11	20	61	104	7	7	16	70	22

☐ The most important attribute in the dimension.

▨ Second most important attribute in the dimension.

☐ Third most important attribute in the dimension.

In this dimension, students in all three programs declared *'Is relevant to job/career'* as the attribute of greatest influence on the effectiveness of transnational computing programs. In all three programs, this attribute was ranked highest overall and in terms of the percentage of first choices – 33%, 34%, and 27% in the corresponding programs.

The other two top attributes selected by students in Program1 were *'Relates the new material to previous student knowledge'* and *'Integrates all course elements into a well-paced package'*.

Students in Program2 and Program3 selected *'Course objectives and learning outcomes are communicated to students'* as their second choice, while the attributes ranked third in the respective programs included *'Integrates all course elements into a well-paced package'* and *'Relates the new material to previous student knowledge'*.

The attributes ranked lowest in this dimension were *'Instructors and students agree on deadlines for completion and marking of assignments'* in Program1 and Program2, and *'Learning objectives are supported by instructional methodologies'* in Program3.

4.4.3.7. Ranking of attributes in the dimension *Interaction*

The ranking of attributes in the dimension *Interaction* is presented in Table 4.4.3.7. Numbers indicating percentages of ranking responses have been rounded to the nearest integer.

Table 4.4.3.7. Dimension *Interaction*: ranking of attributes.

Attribute	Program1 (N=49)					Program2 (N=160)					Program3 (N=45)				
	1st (%)	2nd (%)	3rd (%)	None (%)	Weighted sum	1st (%)	2nd (%)	3rd (%)	None (%)	Weighted sum	1st (%)	2nd (%)	3rd (%)	None (%)	Weighted sum
Timely feedback on assignments and projects.	29	22	14	35	71	37	16	18	29	257	44	24	8	24	85
Involvement in small learning groups.	12	10	25	53	40	8	16	10	66	102	9	7	11	73	23
Use of interactive instructional strategies.	27	29	14	30	74	23	18	16	43	191	27	13	18	42	56
Frequent contact with the instructor.	10	12	10	68	32	9	11	12	68	98	4	11	11	74	21
Use of electronic media and telephone to interact with instructors.	6	16	16	62	33	10	20	16	54	137	4	16	24	56	31
Development of formats and strategies encouraging communication between students, and students and instructors.	16	10	20	54	44	14	19	29	38	175	11	29	29	31	54

The most important attribute in the dimension.

Second most important attribute in the dimension.

Third most important attribute in the dimension.

The ranking of the attributes considered to be of greatest importance in this dimension was very similar in all three programs. While students in all programs gave the greatest number of first choices (29%, 37%, and 44% respectively) to *'Timely feedback on assignments and projects'*, followed by *'Use of interactive instructional strategies'* as the attribute with second highest number of first choices (27% in Program1, 23% in Program2, and 27% in Program3), the order of importance of the two attributes with respect to the overall score – the weighted sum – was reversed in Program1. Students in all three programs selected the same attribute, *'Development of formats and strategies encouraging communication between students, and students and instructors'*, as their third choice.

Students in all programs also selected a common attribute which they considered to be of lowest importance namely, *'Frequent contact with the instructor'*.

4.4.3.8. Ranking of attributes in the dimension *Evaluation and assessment*

The ranking of attributes in the dimension Evaluation and Assessment is presented in Table 4.4.3.8; percentages have been rounded to the nearest integer for clarity of presentation.

Table 4.4.3.8. Dimension *Evaluation and assessment*: ranking of attributes.

Attribute	Program1 (N=49)					Program2 (N=160)					Program3 (N=45)				
	1st (%)	2nd (%)	3rd (%)	None (%)	Weighted sum	1st (%)	2nd (%)	3rd (%)	None (%)	Weighted sum	1st (%)	2nd (%)	3rd (%)	None (%)	Weighted sum
Assessment of students' attitudes and levels of satisfaction.	29	22	20	29	74	28	14	15	43	205	22	13	20	45	51
Assessment of the relevance of course content in practice.	25	27	20	28	72	20	27	24	29	221	18	31	18	33	60
Methods of assessment match learning objectives.	25	25	10	40	65	32	24	27	17	272	40	20	22	18	82
Continuous evaluation of students' academic progress.	16	12	20	52	46	9	22	15	54	139	7	22	20	51	38
Continuous evaluation of the course.	6	14	29	51	37	11	13	19	57	123	13	13	20	54	39

The most important attribute in the dimension.

Second most important attribute in the dimension.

Third most important attribute in the dimension.

The choice of the three most influential attributes in this dimension was the same in all three programs. However, the ranking of the top attributes varied between the programs. Students in Program2 and Program3 ordered the three most influential attributes as follows: *'Methods of assessment match learning objectives'*, *'Assessment of the relevance of the course content in practice'*, and *'Assessment of students' attitudes and levels of satisfaction'*. Students in Program1 ranked *'Assessment of students' attitudes and levels of satisfaction'* highest, followed by *'Assessment of the relevance of the course content in practice'*, and *'Methods of assessment match learning objectives'*.

'Continuous evaluation of the course' and *'Continuous evaluation of students' academic progress'* were ranked lowest in all programs.

4.4.3.9. Ranking of attributes in the dimension *Technology*

The ranking of attributes in the dimension *Technology*, with percentages rounded to the nearest integer, is presented in Table 4.4.3.9.

Table 4.4.3.9. Dimension *Technology*: ranking of attributes.

Attribute	Program1 (N=49)					Program2 (N160)					Program3 (N=45)				
	1st (%)	2nd (%)	3rd (%)	None (%)	Weighted sum	1st (%)	2nd (%)	3rd (%)	None (%)	Weighted sum	1st (%)	2nd (%)	3rd (%)	None (%)	Weighted sum
Current products are used.	29	8	14	49	57	31	13	14	42	210	18	13	24	45	47
Is helpful and easy to use.	31	33	8	28	81	29	29	14	28	254	31	22	11	36	67
Is available and reliable.	20	31	18	31	69	16	29	25	30	210	18	33	22	27	64
Software applications are appropriate and easy to use.	12	16	27	45	47	13	21	26	40	168	20	16	24	40	52
Access to technical assistance throughout the course.	8	10	31	51	37	13	9	19	59	119	13	16	20	51	41

The most important attribute in the dimension.

Second most important attribute in the dimension.

Third most important attribute in the dimension.

Students in all three programs singled out the attribute *'Is helpful and easy to use'* as the most important attribute of technology. *'Is available and reliable'* was a common second choice in all programs, although in Program2 this attribute was tied with *'Current products are used'* in the second place. *'Current products are used'* was ranked third in Program1, whereas in Program3 *'Software applications are appropriate and easy to use'* was placed in third position.

The attribute ranked lowest in all three programs was *'Access to technical assistance throughout the course'*.

4.4.3.10. Ranking of attributes in the dimension *Course management and organisational support*

Finally, students ranked the attributes in the dimension *Course management and organisational support*; the ranking results, with percentages rounded to the nearest integer, are presented in Table 4.4.3.10.

Table 4.4.3.10. Dimension *Course management and organisational support*: ranking of attributes.

Attribute	Program1 (N=49)					Program2 (N=160)					Program3 (N=45)				
	1st (%)	2nd (%)	3rd (%)	None (%)	Weighted sum	1st (%)	2nd (%)	3rd (%)	None (%)	Weighted sum	1st (%)	2nd (%)	3rd (%)	None (%)	Weighted sum
Timely preparation of course materials.	33	6	16	45	62	23	15	17	45	186	27	29	13	31	68
Procedures exist to quickly respond to student complaints.	25	6	14	55	49	21	16	11	52	169	18	13	22	47	46
Institution ensures high quality of the course.	25	41	6	28	79	20	25	16	39	202	4	31	13	52	40
Student support services are provided (e.g. student registration, distribution of materials, ordering of textbooks, processing of examination results).	8	18	27	47	43	16	18	23	43	169	22	13	16	49	49
Training on obtaining information through course Web sites, electronic databases, interlibrary loans, etc. provided.	4	20	18	58	35	9	16	15	60	116	11	7	20	62	30
Effective overall course coordination.	6	8	18	68	26	12	9	18	61	116	18	7	16	59	37

The most important attribute in the dimension.

Second most important attribute in the dimension.

Third most important attribute in the dimension.

Students in Program1 and Program2 ranked the top three attributes in this dimension identically; 'Institution ensures high quality of the course' was ranked first, 'Timely preparation of course materials' second, and 'Procedures exist to quickly respond to student complaints' third. However, in Program2 the third attribute was tied in the third place with 'Student support services are provided'.

Students in Program3 ranked 'Timely preparation of course materials' as the most influential attribute. The other two attributes were 'Student support services are provided' and 'Procedures exist to quickly respond to student complaints'.

While students in Program2 ranked 'Training on obtaining information through course Web sites, electronic databases, interlibrary loans, etc. is provided' and 'Effective overall course coordination' equally lowest, the former attribute was ranked lowest in Program3, while the latter was ranked lowest in Program1.

4.4.3.11. Identification of additional success attributes

In addition to ranking the importance of the predetermined attributes of the multidimensional model, the survey also sought to identify further attributes that might have been absent from the proposed model. To this end, students were asked to give reasons for enrolling in the programs, as well as state if they considered this type of program (offered by an offshore university) worthwhile; students were asked to justify their opinions.

The main reasons for enrolling in the programs included: desire to obtain a higher qualification; opportunity to obtain a degree in as short a time as possible and at a reasonable cost; wish to upgrade existing qualifications while working; program fees cheaper than those charged for similar program provided by a local university; and, recognition of prior learning resulting in course exemptions.

Although students' opinions on the perceived value of transnational programs were divided, a great majority of respondents in all three programs – 79% in Program1, 86% in Program2, and 66% in Program3 – considered this type of program worthwhile; this assessment of the potential value of transnational programs by the students was more favourable than their view of the perceived effectiveness of the programs in which they were currently participating. Table 4.4.3.11 presents a comparison of the perceived effectiveness of current programs and perceived value of transnational programs in general by students in the targeted programs.

Table 4.4.3.11. Comparison of the perceived effectiveness of current programs and perceived value of transnational programs in general (as percentage of students).

	Program 1		Program 2		Program 3	
	Yes	No	Yes	No	Yes	No
Is the current program effective?	85	15	78	22	49	51
Would you participate in this type of program in the future?	69	31	47	53	47	53
Is this type of program (transnational) worthwhile?	79	21	86	14	66	34

Students, who regarded their programs as worthwhile, attributed it to: the opportunity to obtain a University qualification while working full time; competitive program fees; relatively short program duration; recognition of prior qualifications resulting in subject exemptions; and, flexible program structure. Students, who did not regard their programs as worthwhile, cited the following reasons: poor teaching skills of local instructors; lack of adequate feedback on assessment tasks; poor administrative services on the part of the partner institution; and, poor technological support for a computing degree program.

4.4.3.12. Responses to hypotheses (1) – (4)

Part B of the survey was used to test hypotheses regarding student perceptions of critical success attributes of transnational computing programs. The data for hypotheses (1) through (4) was collected from students participating in the evaluated programs, and the results presented in Sections 4.4.3.1 through to 4.4.3.10. This section summarises responses to the abovementioned hypotheses. Further discussion on the relevance of these results to the refinement of the multidimensional model is presented in Section 4.6.

Hypothesis (1):

Critical success attributes (of effective distance education programs) in each dimension will be evident in each targeted transnational program.

This hypothesis was supported. As evidenced by the validation results, students perceived every attribute in each of the ten dimensions as important to the effectiveness of the transnational programs although some attributes, such as, for example, the attribute 'Develops effective graphics' in the Instructor – Technology and organisation dimension, barely registered.

Hypothesis (2):

Some attributes will be regarded as more important to the success of transnational programs than others.

This hypothesis was also supported. In every dimension, students in each of the evaluated programs nominated between one and three attributes as particularly important to the success of the programs. The support of the hypothesis was strengthened by the fact that there was a great degree of agreement on these critical attributes between the students in the three evaluated programs. In each of the programs, three attributes ranked highest in each dimension were used for comparative analysis between the programs. Table 4.4.3.12.a presents a summary of this analysis; in each dimension, only attributes ranked among the highest three in at least two programs are listed.

Table 4.4.3.12.a. Students' perceptions of critical success attributes.
(Only attributes selected as most important by students in at least two programs are listed).

Dimension	Attribute	Program
Student	Is motivated and self-disciplined.	1,2,3
	Has positive attitude towards technology-based learning.	1,2,3
University instructor and learning environment	Understands course requirements, students' characteristics and needs.	1,2,3
	Uses effective communication skills.	2,3
	Encourages communication between students, and students and instructors.	1,2,3
Hong Kong instructor and learning environment	Understands course requirements, students' characteristics and needs.	1,2,3
	Uses effective communication skills.	1,2,3
	Encourages communication between students, and students and instructors.	1,2,3
University instructor – Technology and organisation	Is well prepared and organised.	1,2,3
	Provides well designed syllabus and presentation outlines.	1,2,3
	Has experience with technology-based courses.	2,3
Hong Kong instructor – Technology and organisation	Is well prepared and organised.	1,2,3
	Has experience with technology-based courses.	1,2,3
	Provides well designed syllabus and presentation outlines.	2,3
Curriculum and instruction design	Is relevant to job/career.	1,2,3
	Course objectives and learning outcomes are clearly communicated.	2,3
	Relates the new material to previous student knowledge.	1,3
	Integrates all course elements into a well-paced package.	1,2
Interaction	Timely feedback on assignments and projects.	1,2,3
	Use of interactive instructional strategies.	1,2,3
	Strategies that encourage communication between students, and students and instructors.	1,2,3
Evaluation and assessment	Methods of assessment match learning objectives.	1,2,3
	Assessment of the relevance of course content in practice.	1,2,3
	Assessment of students' attitudes and levels of satisfaction.	1,2,3
Technology	Is helpful and easy to use.	1,2,3
	Is available and reliable.	1,2,3
	Current products are used.	1,2
Course management and organisational support	Timely preparation of course materials.	1,2,3
	Institution ensures high quality of the course.	1,2
	Student support services are provided.	2,3
	Procedures exist to quickly respond to student complaints.	1,2,3

☐ The most important attribute in a dimension.

Figure 4.4.3.12.a presents the dimensions of the model (as initially depicted in Figure 4.2.1 in Section 4.2.1.) together with the single most important attribute in each dimension. Since the same attributes were regarded as most important with respect to both University and Hong Kong instructors, the instructor related dimensions of *Instructor and learning environment* and *Instructor – Technology and organisation* include both types of instructors.

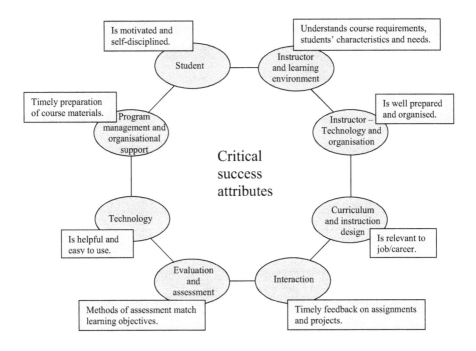

Figure 4.4.3.12.a. Most important attributes of the multidimensional model.

Some of the attributes in the dimensions were perceived by the students as moderately, or barely, important. In this instance also there was a great degree of overlap in the perceptions of students from the evaluated programs. In each of the programs, two attributes ranked lowest in each dimension were used for comparative analysis between the programs. Table 4.4.3.12.b presents a summary of this analysis; in each dimension, only attributes ranked lowest and second lowest in at least two programs are listed.

Table 4.4.3.12.b. Students' perceptions of the least important success attributes.
(Only attributes selected as least important by students in at least two programs are listed).

Dimension	Attribute	Program
Student	Is willing to ask instructors for assistance.	1,2,3
	Is involved and participates.	1,2,3
University instructor and learning environment	Ensures student support services.	1,2,3
	Encourages students to take responsibility for their own learning.	1,2,3
Hong Kong instructor and learning environment	Ensures student support services.	1,2,3
	Conducts students' needs assessment and course evaluation.	1,2,3
University instructor – Technology and organisation	Develops effective graphics.	1,2,3
	Demonstrates control over technology.	1,2,3
Hong Kong instructor – Technology and organisation	Develops effective graphics.	1,2,3
	Is proficient in instructional design.	1,2,3
Curriculum and instruction design	Instructors and students agree on deadlines for completion and marking of assignments.	1,2
	Learning objectives are supported by instructional methodologies.	1,2,3
Interaction	Frequent contact with the instructor.	1,2,3
	Involvement in small groups.	2,3
Evaluation and assessment	Continuous evaluation of the program.	1,2,3
	Continuous evaluation of students' academic progress.	1,2,3
Technology	Access to technical assistance throughout the program.	1,2,3
	Software applications are appropriate and easy to use.	1,2
Course management and organisational support	Effective overall program coordination.	1,2
	Training on obtaining information through program Web sites, electronic databases, interlibrary loans, etc. provided.	1,2,3

[ ] The least important attribute in a dimension.

Figure 4.4.3.12.b presents the dimensions of the model (as initially depicted in Figure 4.2.1 in Section 4.2.1.) together with the single least important attribute in each dimension. Since the same attributes were regarded as least important with respect to both University and Hong Kong instructors, the instructor related dimensions of *Instructor and learning environment* and *Instructor – Technology and organisation* include both types of instructors. In addition, as there was no consensus between the students in all three programs regarding the least important attribute in the dimensions *Curriculum and instructional design*, and *Course management and organisational support*, no "least important" attributes have been depicted for those dimensions.

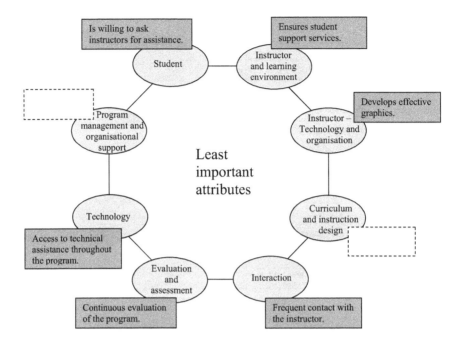

Figure 4.4.3.12.b. Least important attributes of the multidimensional model.

Hypothesis (3):

    Additional attributes, not included in the current dimensional model, will be identified as critical to the effectiveness of transnational programs.

This hypothesis was supported. Three additional attributes have been identified as important to the effectiveness of transnational programs: relatively short duration of the program, competitive program fees, and liberal exemptions based on recognition of prior learning. It should be noted that these attributes meet the definition of program effectiveness used in this study namely – the distance learning program meets the participants' individual needs and the participant would take another program with the same design (Merisotis & Phipps, 1999).

Hypothesis (4):

In each of the targeted programs, attributes regarded as important with respect to University instructor, will be also regarded as important with respect to local instructor.

This hypothesis was supported. Students in each of the evaluated programs nominated the same critical success attributes for University instructors and Hong Kong instructors alike in the two dimensions pertaining to instructors: *Instructor and learning environment*, and *Instructor – Technology and organisation*. Although there were some differences with respect to the level of importance assigned to the critical attributes between the programs, and between University and Hong Kong instructors within individual programs, appreciation of course requirements and students' needs, effective communication skills, and encouragement of communication between students, and students and instructors were valued highly. These instructor attributes were perceived as the most influential to the effectiveness of the program with respect to all instructors regardless of their affiliation and location. Similarly, students in all three programs regarded preparedness and organisation, experience with technology-based courses, and provision of well-designed syllabus as critical success attributes with respect to both University and Hong Kong instructors. A summary of results used in testing hypothesis (4) is presented in tables 4.4.3.2 through to 4.4.3.5. Table 4.4.3.12.c presents a comparison of attributes regarded as important with respect to University instructor and Hong Kong instructor in Program1.

Table 4.4.3.12.c. Program1: importance of instructor related attributes.

Dimension	Rank	Attribute
University instructor and learning environment	1st	Understands course requirements, students' characteristics and needs.
	2nd	Encourages communication between students, and students and instructors.
	3rd	Conducts students' needs assessement and course evaluation.
Hong Kong instructor and learning environment	1st	Understands course requirements, students' characteristics and needs.
	2nd	Uses effective communication skills.
	3rd	Encourages communication between students, and students and instructors.
University instructor – Technology and organisation	1st	Is well prepared and organised.
	2nd	Provides well designed syllabus and presentation outlines.
	3rd	Has positive attitude towards technology.
Hong Kong instructor – Technology and organisation	1st	Is well prepared and organised.
	2nd	Has experience with technology-based courses.
	3rd	Adapts course materials for delivery through electronic media.

Table 4.4.3.12.d presents the comparison of attributes regarded as important with respect to University instructor and Hong Kong instructor in Program2.

Table 4.4.3.12.d. Program2: importance of instructor related attributes.

Dimension	Rank	Attribute
University instructor and learning environment	1st	Understands course requirements, students' characteristics and needs.
	2nd	Uses effective communication skills.
	3rd	Encourages communication between students, and students and instructors.
Hong Kong instructor and learning environment	1st	Understands course requirements, students' characteristics and needs.
	2nd	Uses effective communication skills.
	3rd	Encourages communication between students, and students and instructors.
University instructor – Technology and organisation	1st	Is well prepared and organised.
	2nd	Has experience with technology-based courses.
	3rd	Provides well-designed syllabus and presentation outlines.
Hong Kong instructor – Technology and organisation	1st	Is well prepared and organised.
	2nd	Has experience with technology-based courses.
	3rd	Provides well-designed syllabus and presentation outlines.

Table 4.4.3.12.e presents the comparison of attributes regarded as important with respect to University instructor and local instructor in Program3.

Table 4.4.3.12.e. Program3: importance of instructor related attributes.

Dimension	Rank	Attribute
University instructor and learning environment	1st	Uses effective communication skills.
	2nd	Understands course requirements, students' characteristics and needs.
	3rd	Encourages communication between students, and students and instructors.
Hong Kong instructor and learning environment	1st	Uses effective communication skills.
	2nd	Understands course requirements, students' characteristics and needs.
	3rd	Encourages communication between students, and students and instructors.
University instructor – Technology and organisation	1st	Provides well-designed syllabus and presentation outlines.
	2nd	Is well prepared and organised.
	3rd	Has experience with technology-based courses.
Hong Kong instructor – Technology and organisation	1st	Is well prepared and organised.
	2nd	Provides well-designed syllabus and presentation outlines.
	3rd	Has experience with technology-based courses.

4.4.4. Attitude towards fully online provision of the programs – Response to hypothesis (9)

In addition to obtaining students' views on critical success attributes of transnational programs, their attitudes towards fully online provision of such programs was also sought. Students did not support fully online provision of the programs. The lack of support was pronounced and ranged from total rejection (100% of students rejected the idea) of online programs by students in Program1, to a marginal support of 9% and 13% in Program2 and Program3 respectively. Students repeatedly stated the importance of face-to-face communication as the most important reason for preferring the current program model. Face-to-face communication was preferred as, according to the respondents, it offered instant feedback, afforded easier communication with fellow students and instructors, was better suited to the resolution of study problems, and gave better motivation to study. Some students were of the view that learning in front of the computer only was too 'cold' and too difficult, while others were of the opinion that Hong Kong people had traditional attitudes towards education and therefore face-to-face communication was more suitable for Hong Kong students. Respondents did, however, acknowledge the usefulness of the Internet as a means for provision of course material and communication with instructors and fellow students.

Hypothesis (9):

Transnational programs based on face-to-face delivery mode will be preferred by students to programs delivered fully online.

This hypothesis was supported. As evidenced by the results presented above, students were overwhelmingly in favour of the current model of their programs, that is programs that were based on face-to-face communication and used the Internet for support.

4.5. OUTCOMES OF GROUP INTERVIEWS WITH STUDENTS

Prior to the group interviews, the survey results were examined to determine if there was a need to clarify any issues that might have arisen as a consequence of the survey. Results of the survey indicated that there was a difference in responses depending on the program. Therefore, the questions for the group interviews were designed to broaden the researcher's understanding of the targeted programs (Appendix C).

A total of forty-four students participated in six group interviews: one session with seven students from Program 1; four sessions with twenty-nine students from Program2; and, one session with eight students from Program3. The results from the interviews are reported below. To ensure anonymity, participating students are identified only by their program identifier; that is, S1 refers to a student in Program1, S2 identifies a student in Program2, and S3 points to a student in Program3.

The collected results have been grouped into four themes: factors influencing students' decision about enrolling in a transnational program; students' perceptions regarding program effectiveness; students' views on potential fully online provision of the program; and, students' suggestions for program improvement. The results are reported in the following four subsections.

4.5.1. Factors influencing student decisions about enrolment

The survey identified three additional program attributes that students regarded as important to the effectiveness of transnational programs: relatively short duration of the program, competitive program fees, and liberal exemptions based on recognition of prior learning. To confirm this survey finding in the interviews with students, one of the interview questions was, "What made you decide to enroll in the program?" Students listed several reasons that shaped their decisions about enrolment including: a desire to obtain a university degree while working at the same time; and, a need to upgrade their qualifications to further their career prospects, or change careers. However, first, in the order of importance, students nominated competitive program fees, access to the program and favourable entry requirements, and relatively short duration of the program. The latter three reasons reported by the students confirmed the corresponding survey findings; these reasons were reported by students from all the evaluated programs.

This course was a perfect fit for my qualifications, and the course fee was reasonable – I could afford it (S1).

The course fee was important, it was cheaper than the fee charged by Open University Hong Kong, and it was a fixed fee. So, from the very beginning of the course I knew how much it would cost me to complete it, I could "control the project" (S1).

The fixed fee was important. In Hong Kong various institutions charge different fees every year. I did not want surprises (S1).

The course fee is fixed for four years, so I can budget for my studies (S1).

I wanted to get a degree at a reasonable price. The fee for this course is reasonable. The courses at local universities are much more expensive, too expensive for me (S2).

I did not want to enrol in a course at a Hong Kong university because it was much more expensive, and much more time consuming. At the Open University, for example, a degree in Computer Science takes seven years to complete (S2).

This course has a reasonable fee and is short enough (S2).

Even with government support, a degree in Computer Science can cost anything between HKD 100K and 120K at a local university. It is too expensive for me. So this course is very cheap in comparison (S2).

This course is better than a local (Hong Kong) one because it is cheap and short. It only takes two years to complete the course and the fee is cheap (S3).

With my IVE diploma, it would still take me three or four years to complete the degree at a Hong Kong university. This course is quicker and much cheaper than a similar course at the Hong Kong Polytechnic or Open University Hong Kong (S3).

I could meet the entry requirements for this course (S1).

There is a quota on the number of available places at the local universities; I could not get in even if I wanted to (S2).

4.5.2. Perceptions of program effectiveness

Results from the survey indicated differences between the programs in the level of satisfaction with the current programs and in the perception of program effectiveness. Accordingly, questions were asked during the group interviews to expand the researcher's understanding of factors influencing the differences. First, students were asked about the extent to which the program met their expectations. Some students replied to this question using percentages; the percentages for Program1 were between

70% and 80%; 70% for Program2; and, 50-70% for Program3. Students in all programs approved of the theoretical but pointed out the inadequacy of the practical component of the programs:

The theoretical part of IT is O.K., but the practical part is not sufficient (S1).

We did not learn enough to be able to design Web sites; we did not practise that, and Web site design is important in business, IT, and e-commerce (S1).

The material is very theoretical; there is not enough practice (S2).

The theory is fine, but the technical application is missing. We know the theory, but not how to apply it in practice. How can I build a database in Oracle for example (S2)?

There are not enough practical programming assignments (S3).

It would be good to have a test lab for a subject like Networks and Communications (S3).

Students in Program1 reported being overwhelmed by the number of assignments (and the associated workload) that they were expected to complete in every subject of the program:

We are part-time students, we work full time. The amount of work required by assignments is difficult to handle. There are on average three assignments in every subject, and this is a lot of work (S1).

The assignments are worth 50% of the final mark. There should be fewer assignments (S1).

I would still like assignments, not just the final examination, but I would like fewer assignments, say one or two, and they could still be worth 50% of the final mark (S1).

Students in Program2 and Program3 reported that the administrative support in handling assignments was inadequate:

Handing in assignments is a problem sometimes, because we have to hand them in during office hours, but we work full-time (S2).

Sometimes, I have to take time off work to hand in assignments (S3).

Students were also asked to indicate which aspects of the program, if any, they would like enhanced or reduced. Students unanimously responded that they would like more opportunities for hands-on experience:

More practical application of IT (S1).

More practical Web development (S1).

More practical software, system, database applications, and Internet applications development (S2).

I would like to learn how to apply the computing knowledge in practice (S2).

More practical, job-related exercises (S3).

On the other hand, students would like fewer assignments; they would also like some subjects, such as mathematics and statistics, removed from the program:

We would like fewer assignments (S1).

No Discrete Mathematics (S2).

No Forecasting, Statistics, or Simulation (S2).

There should not be subjects like mathematics in the course; they are a waste of time (S3).

4.5.3. Views on fully online program provision

Results from the survey revealed that students opposed fully online provision of transnational programs and were adamant about the importance of face-to-face contact with both lecturers and fellow students. One of the questions in the group interviews addressed this issue again to explore further the reasons behind the students' views. Students again responded in favour of the current model of the programs, that is one with a substantial face-to-face component. They regarded face-to-face communication as: more conducive to the learning process; affording better opportunity to share knowledge and ask for help; and, "easier" and more interactive.

Face-to-face; there is more opportunity to talk to the lecturer (S1).

We humans are lazy. It is easier to talk to the lecturer than learn from the computer. I also want face-to-face communication with my friends (fellow students) (S1).

Face-to-face, because you can ask for explanation if you do not understand; it is quicker and easier to ask than find the answer online (S2).

It is important to have the support of friends in the course. We often study together, or if I do not know something, I can ask my friend (S2).

It is important to share knowledge, and it is better to do it face-to-face (S2).

Face-to-face, because it is interactive (S3).

I prefer face-to-face interaction with both lectures and students. Even if an online course was cheaper, I would still prefer face-to-face (S3).

I could not rely on self-paced learning alone, I need pressure. Otherwise, I would be too lazy to study. It helps if I have to come to classes (S3).

However, students welcomed the Internet as a means for providing course material, facilitating submission of assignments, and enabling communication with lecturers outside classes.

But online support is important, for example course material or email; but only as an addition to face-to-face classes (S1).

Internet is good to provide material, but classes should be face-to-face (S2).

4.5.4. Suggested program improvements

This research study aimed to determine the particular attributes that increase the effectiveness of distance education programs. Results from the survey indicated which aspects of such programs are important to students. However, the success aspects identified though the survey were predetermined and therefore generic. To further the understanding of student choices with respect to critical success factors, students were asked what advice they would give to the University offering their programs. Students' recommendations focused on: increasing the teaching involvement of University lecturers; enhancing the practical component of the programs; and, reviewing assessment strategies:

It would be good to increase the number of classes taught by Australian lectures to six per subject. It would be half of the subject. They teach only four classes presently (S1).

It would be good to have an online discussion group or a chat room involving Australian lecturers, especially before examinations (S2).

I would prefer if the Australian lecturers taught half of the course. Half/half would be fair (S3).

Enhance the IT part of the course in terms of both the depth and the width (breadth) (S1).

We need more emphasis on Internet technologies and practical Web design. IT changes very rapidly all the time and we need to develop technical skills, new technical skills (S1).

I think that the course should focus more on technology and technical skills, and subjects such as Networks and Communications, Java, Internet, and not statistics or simulation (S2).

We need more practice. This is a computing course, so when I apply for a computing job, my employer would prefer a graduate with good technical skills (S3).

The course should have more practical system development (S3).

We should have fewer assignments. And assignments should be group assignments, so that we could share ideas and work together (S1).

There should be a change in the assessment structure. Currently, there is too much focus on the final examination. Assignments should be worth more, possibly 50% of the final mark; 50% assignments, 50% examination (S2).

4.6. REVISION OF THE MULTIDIMENSIONAL MODEL

Following the evaluation of the multidimensional model through surveys and interviews with students in three transnational computing programs, the original model, detailed in Sections 4.2.1 and 4.2.2, has been refined to incorporate the results of the validation. The refinement involved four changes: first, the distinction between University and Hong Kong instructors in the two instructor-related dimensions

Instructor and learning environment and *Instructor – technology and organisation* was removed; second, a new dimension, called *Pre-enrolment considerations*, was introduced to the model; third, the least important attributes were removed from the model; and, last, the attributes in each dimension were listed according to their perceived importance.

4.6.1. Revision of instructor-related dimensions

Since the transnational education programs involve both university instructors as well as instructors of the partner institutions, the original instructor-related dimensions *Instructor and learning environment* and *Instructor – technology and organisation* were initially further divided into *University instructor and learning environment* and *Hong Kong instructor and learning environment*, and *University instructor – Technology and organisation* and *Hong Kong instructor – technology and organisation* respectively; this extension of the two instructor-related dimensions was motivated by the need to distinguish between the effectiveness of instructors from offering university and the partner institution.

One of the hypotheses in this study, hypothesis (4), tested if attributes regarded as important with respect to University instructors would also be regarded as important with respect to local instructors. This hypothesis was supported, as reported in Section 4.4.3.12. In view of this result, the distinction between University and Hong Kong instructor proved to be unnecessary, and the multidimensional model was amended accordingly.

4.6.2. Introduction of a new dimension: *Pre-enrolment considerations*

One purpose of the validation of the multidimensional model was to check if any additional attributes, not included in the original model, would be identified by students as critical to the effectiveness of transnational programs; this test was the subject of hypothesis (3) in this study. This hypothesis was supported, as reported in Section 4.4.3.12. As revealed by the survey results in Section 4.4.3.11, and further confirmed by the results obtained from group interviews with students in Section 4.5.1, students identified three additional attributes contributing to program effectiveness: competitive program fees; relatively short program duration; and, recognition of prior qualifications resulting in subject exemptions.

The new attributes could not be placed in any of the original dimensions of the model as they fell outside of their realm. Although not compatible with any of the existing dimensions, the new attributes shared an important property – they were regarded by the students prior to enrolling in the program. It was decided that a new dimension, called *Pre-enrolment considerations*, should be introduced to the model, and that this dimension should include the newly identified attributes. Figure 4.6.2 depicts the refined multidimensional model inclusive of the newly created dimension.

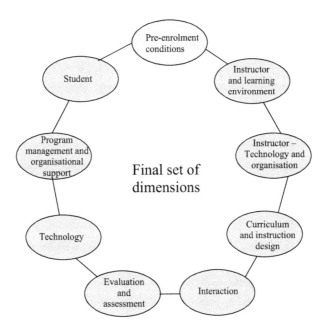

Figure 4.6.2. Multidimensional model – final set of dimensions.

4.6.3. Removal of the least important attributes

The attributes included in the multidimensional model have all been reported in literature as contributors to the effectiveness of distance education programs. However, it was expected that not all of the attributes would be perceived by students as equally critical. Hypothesis (2) in this study sought to confirm that some attributes would be regarded as more important to the success of transnational programs than others. This hypothesis was supported, as reported in Section 4.4.3.12.

While several attributes in each dimension were regarded by students as critically important, other attributes in the dimensions were perceived by the students as moderately, or barely, important. In this instance also there was a great degree of overlap in the perceptions of students from the evaluated programs. It was therefore considered to be of limited benefit to retain in the model the attributes ranked lowest in all three evaluated programs; consequently, these attributes were removed from the original model. It should be noted that no attributes were removed from the dimensions *Curriculum and instructional design*, and *Course management and organisational support*, as there was no consensus between the students in all three programs regarding the least important attribute. No attributes were removed from the newly introduced dimension of *Pre-enrolment considerations*, as the attributes within this dimension had not been ranked by the students. Table 4.6.3 presents a summary of the removed attributes across the dimensions of the model.

Table 4.6.3. Removed attributes: attributes perceived as least important in all evaluated programs.

Dimension	Least important attribute	Program
Student	Is willing to ask instructors for assistance.	1,2,3
Instructor and learning environment	Ensures student support services.	1,2,3
Instructor – Technology and organisation	Develops effective graphics.	1,2,3
Curriculum and instruction design	None	
Interaction	Frequent contact with the instructor.	1,2,3
Evaluation and assessment	Continuous evaluation of the program.	1,2,3
Technology	Access to technical assistance throughout the program.	1,2,3
Course management and organisational support	None	
Pre-enrolment considerations	None	

4.6.4. Refined version of the multidimensional model

As indicated in the previous section (Section 4.6.3), and confirmed by hypothesis (2) in this study (Section 4.4.3.12), some attributes of the multidimensional model were regarded as more important to the success of transnational programs than others. Consequently, it was decided that to better reflect the perceived importance of the attributes within each dimension of the model, they ought to be listed according to their perceived importance. Table 4.6.4 presents the refined version of the original model incorporating all the changes discussed in this section and section 4.6.1 – 4.6.3.

Table 4.6.4. Multidimensional model for transnational computing education programs – final version (attributes are listed in order of importance).

Dimension	Attribute
Student	Is motivated and self-disciplined. Has positive attitude towards technology-based learning. Works as a team player. Knows how to work independently. Is confident in using technology. Is involved and participates.
Instructor and learning environment	Understands course requirements, students' characteristics and needs. Uses effective communication skills. Encourages communication between students, and students and instructors. Demonstrates dedication to the course, teaching and students. Encourages students to take responsibility for their own learning. Conducts students' needs assessment and course evaluation.
Instructor – Technology and organisation	Is well prepared and organised. Provides well designed syllabus and presentation outlines. Has experience with technology-based courses. Adapts course materials for delivery through electronic media. Has positive attitude towards technology. Is proficient in instructional design. Uses interactive instructional strategies. Demonstrates control over technology.
Curriculum and instruction design	Is relevant to job/career. Course objectives and learning outcomes are clearly communicated. Relates the new material to previous student knowledge. Integrates all course elements into a well-paced package. Creates logical sequences for each element presented. Learning objectives are supported by instructional methodologies. Instructors and students agree on deadlines for completion/marking of assignments.
Interaction	Timely feedback on assignments and projects. Use of interactive instructional strategies. Strategies that encourage communication between students, and students and instructors. Use of electronic media and telephone to interact with instructors. Involvement in small learning groups.
Evaluation and assessment	Methods of assessment match learning objectives. Assessment of the relevance of course content in practice. Assessment of students' attitudes and levels of satisfaction. Continuous evaluation of students' academic progress.
Technology	Is helpful and easy to use. Is available and reliable. Current products are used. Software applications are appropriate and easy to use.
Course management and organisational support	Timely preparation of course materials. Institution ensures high quality of the course. Student support services are provided. Procedures exist to quickly respond to student complaints. Training is provided on obtaining information through course Web sites, electronic databases, library, etc. Effective overall course coordination.
Pre-enrolment considerations	Competitive course fees. Short course duration. Subject exemptions for prior qualifications.

4.7. CONCLUSION

This chapter has presented the conclusion to the development and validation of a conceptual model for transnational computing education programs. This model takes into consideration various dimensions of the distance education context, instead of focusing exclusively on technology. The dimensions, relevant particularly to transnational education, include student attributes and practices, instructor attributes and practices, curriculum and instruction design, interaction, evaluation and assessment, technological attributes, and program management and organisational support. This chapter detailed the dimensions of the model together with their attributes.

The model was applied to three transnational computing programs for validation. The results of the validation supported the original premise that technology represents but one dimension of the distance education context and, that other dimensions also contribute to the effectiveness of distance education programs. The results also showed that the transnational students, irrespective of the evaluated program, agreed on the aspects that they considered most important to the effectiveness of transnational programs. Among all the aspects across all the dimensions in all programs, three were singled out as the most influential of all: instructors' preparation for, and organisation of, classes; relevance of the program with respect to job/career; and, instructors' appreciation of program requirements, students' characteristics and needs.

While the evaluation of the multidimensional model confirmed the inclusion of all the attributes in the existing dimensions (every attribute was rated as at least 'somewhat important', albeit by very few respondents), it also identified other attributes, not included in the original model, that students considered critical to program effectiveness. These attributes included program cost, duration, and extent of recognition for prior qualifications.

Finally, the original model was revised to incorporate the results of the validation and a refined version of the model has been developed. The refined model includes the additional success attributes identified by the students; it excludes the attributes that were declared as least important by students in all programs; and, within each dimension, it presents the attributes in their perceived order of importance.

Chapter 5 outlines the conclusions and limitations related to the multidimensional model, implications of the research, and recommendations for future research related to transnational education programs.

Chapter 5

CONCLUSIONS AND RECOMMENDATIONS

5.1. INTRODUCTION

With rapid expansion of the transnational education market, more and more universities join the ranks of transnational education providers, or expand their transnational education offerings. This study has developed a conceptual model for transnational computing education programs using student perceptions as a framework. This model allows academics involved in teaching, managing, and developing such programs to gain insights into program effectiveness as perceived by transnational students.

This chapter begins with a summary of my thesis in Section 5.2, with each chapter summarised. Section 5.3 addresses the major findings of my study, followed by Section 5.4 that describes three major contributions of my study. The constraints and limitations of my study are summarised in Section 5.5, whereas Section 5.6 outlines recommendations for future research related to my study.

5.2. OVERVIEW OF THE THESIS

The first chapter of this thesis provides a general background to the evolution of distance and transnational education, in addition to the aims and significance of this study. The overview of distance and transnational education (Section 1.1) focuses on tertiary education, its rapid expansion, and the need for educational providers to offer good quality programs to attract students. I highlight the need for universities to acknowledge, and respond to, student needs, even more so since the competition for students in the transnational education arena has become more intense. I also underline the need for investigation of quality and effectiveness of transnational programs in addition to their technological aspects. I present a brief introduction to the effectiveness of distance/transnational education and identify the research problem and hypotheses (Section 1.2), followed by an outline of methods and significance of this study (Sections 1.3 & 1.4). The aims of my study are: (1) to investigate attributes that may determine the effectiveness of distance education programs in general, and transnational computing programs in particular; (2) to use these attributes to develop a conceptual model for effective transnational programs; and, (3) to apply the model to selected transnational computing programs for validation. Finally, I point out that this study is significant in three ways. First, in terms of transnational education, this study expands on current and past transnational education research. Second, in terms of contributing to knowledge regarding effectiveness of transnational education programs, it incorporates student perspective into the program effectiveness framework. Third, by determining specific attributes of effective transnational programs, it provides a model to assist in making informed decisions in the design, development, and review of transnational programs.

Chapter 2 provides a review of literature in five areas related to the study: (1) the evolution of distance education; (2) the impact of technology on distance education; (3) the transnational education model; (4) requirements of computing education at a distance; and, (5) distance education effectiveness. The major section concerning the evolution of distance education (Section 2.2) discusses the history and transformation of distance education to create a framework for the sequence of events that have contributed to the distance education movements and shaped modern post-secondary distance education programs. Section 2.3 explores the fundamental role that technology has played in the evolution and growth of distance education. Section 2.4 focuses on one type of distance education, which is the subject of this research study – transnational education. It discusses the definition of transnational education and its subtype: the Australian transnational education. The typology of transnational education is also reviewed, as are factors determining demand and supply, and characteristics of typical programs. The section concludes with a discussion on the role that face-to-face interaction plays in transnational programs. The next section (Section 2.5) highlights the particular demands of teaching computing programs in a transnational setting: firstly, the need to update study material in a rapidly changing discipline; secondly, the requirement to teach subjects involving theory, higher analytical reasoning, and problem solving; and finally, the demand to accommodate hardware and software needs of the students. Section 2.6 links distance education with student satisfaction and effectiveness of distance education programs, especially in terms of tertiary education. Finally, as this research study involved investigation of critical success factors in transnational education programs, Section 2.7 reviews in detail the factors that define effectiveness of those programs; it examines attributes of distance education students, instructors, technology, program design, and organisational support that contribute to program effectiveness.

Chapter 3 describes the approach that I used to develop and validate the multidimensional model for transnational education programs; it describes the research design, the population and sample, instrumentation, data collection, and data analyses that were used in the study. Section 3.2 outlines methods used in the development and validation of the multidimensional model. The development of the model was a two-step process. Firstly, success attributes of distance education programs, with emphasis on transnational programs, were identified. Secondly, these attributes were grouped into broader categories – dimensions; this collection of dimensions formed a model of effective transnational programs. Two methods of data collection (a survey and group interviews), and multiple data sources (three transnational computing programs) were used to validate the model; Section 3.3 provides a description of those data sources. Sections 3.4 & 3.5 describe the means by which the data was collected,

143

as well as the ethical considerations associated with data collection. Finally, Section 3.6 describes the methods used for the analysis of data.

Chapter 4 presents the conclusion to the development and validation of the multidimensional model. First, Section 4.2 details the dimensions of the proposed model including: *Student*, *Instructor and learning environment*, *Instructor – Technology and support*, *Curriculum and instruction design*, *Interaction*, *Evaluation and assessment*, *Technology*, and *Program management and organisational support*. Second, Section 4.3 describes the three transnational computing education programs used for validation of the model; the programs are offered by Australian universities to students in Hong Kong. Third, Sections 4.4 & 4.5 present the results of model validation through the survey and group interviews with students. Finally, following validation, the refined version of the model is presented in Section 4.6; the refinement involved the introduction of a new dimension, *Pre-enrolment considerations*, removal of least important attributes, and ordering of attributes within dimensions in terms of importance. Chapter 4 also provides responses to the research hypotheses tested in this study.

5.3. MAJOR FINDINGS

This research study had three goals. First, I set out to identify from literature success attributes of distance education programs. Second, based on the identified attributes, I developed a model for effective distance education programs (with emphasis on transnational programs). Finally, I validated the model against three transnational programs, and refined the original model. The following hypotheses guided the analysis of data:

1. Critical success attributes (of effective distance education programs) in each dimension will be evident in each targeted transnational program.

2. Some attributes will be regarded as more important to the success of transnational programs than others.

3. Additional attributes, not included in the current dimensional model, will be identified as critical to the effectiveness of transnational programs.

4. In each of the targeted programs, attributes regarded as important with respect to University instructor, will be also regarded as important with respect to local instructor.

5. For each of the targeted programs, there will be no significant difference in the level of student satisfaction with the University instructor and the local instructor.

6. There will be no significant difference in the level of student satisfaction with transnational programs offered by the same University.

7. There will be no significant difference in the level of student satisfaction with transnational programs operated by the same offshore provider.

8. Each of the targeted transnational programs will be perceived by its students as effective.

9. Transnational programs based on face-to-face delivery mode will be preferred by students to programs delivered fully online.

Three transnational computing programs, which are offered in Hong Kong by Australian universities, in co-operation with Hong Kong partner institutions, participated in the evaluation of the multidimensional model. Data was collected through a survey administered to approximately three hundred students (two hundred and fifty nine useable surveys were returned), and through group interviews with students (forty four students took part in six group interviews).

The following sections describe the major findings stemming from the development and validation of the multidimensional model including responses to the hypotheses tested in this study.

5.3.1. Investigation of student perceptions of the evaluated transnational programs

The transnational programs participating in this study were examined in terms of perceived student satisfaction with several aspects of the program, including: instructors, technology, program management and coordination, and overall program effectiveness. In addition, students' attitude towards the current mode of program provision (predominantly face-to-face) was also assessed.

Satisfaction with instructors in the evaluated programs was high, but it did not apply uniformly to both University and local instructors. On the contrary, there were significant differences in the levels of satisfaction with the two types of instructors in each of the programs, as confirmed by the conclusion to Hypothesis (5):

> For each of the targeted programs, there will be no significant difference in the level of student satisfaction with the University instructor and the local instructor.

This hypothesis was not supported. Findings in two out of three evaluated programs did not support the hypothesis in terms of overall satisfaction with instructors. Students in those programs reported a significantly higher level of overall satisfaction with the University instructors. They were also significantly more satisfied with most individual aspects of University instructors' performance including teaching ability, and organisation and preparation for classes. On the other hand, students in the remaining program were overall more satisfied with local instructors, but not significantly. They were also more satisfied with the local instructors with respect to all individual aspects; significant differences were found regarding instructors' organisation and preparation for classes, dedication to students and teaching, and telephone/email accessibility outside of classes.

Slow feedback on assessment tasks emerged as a major problem in all evaluated programs. Students identified the tardiness with which tests and written assignments were marked and returned as the least satisfactory aspect associated with instructors and instruction. In addition, it was determined that electronic media were not sufficiently used for assignment submission and feedback.

Inadequate access to the university library and other student resources was identified as another major shortcoming of the programs. Students' dissatisfaction with their ability to access vital study resources was pronounced in all three evaluated programs.

Technology used in the programs was highly regarded as useful and easy to use; satisfaction with the overall usefulness of program Web sites was also high. On the other hand, the quality of the available technical support was found to be lacking.

Programs offered by the same University lacked consistency in the levels of student satisfaction with the programs, as confirmed by the conclusion to Hypothesis (6):

> There will be no significant difference in the level of student satisfaction with transnational programs offered by the same University.

To test this hypothesis, data on student satisfaction with all aspects of the program was analysed for two programs offered by the same University, but in co-operation with different offshore partners. This hypothesis was not supported; a comparison of the average student satisfaction scores between the programs produced a significant difference.

Likewise, programs supported by the same offshore partner institution lacked uniformity with respect to student satisfaction with the programs; this was confirmed by the conclusion to Hypothesis (7):

> There will be no significant difference in the level of student satisfaction with transnational programs operated by the same offshore provider.

To test this hypothesis, student satisfaction data was analysed for two transnational programs operated by the same offshore provider, but offered by different universities. This hypothesis was not supported; a significant difference was reported as a result of a comparison of average student satisfaction scores between the programs.

The evaluated transnational programs were not perceived by their students as effective. Program effectiveness was measured in two ways: one, students deemed their current program effective/non-effective; and two, students stated if they would be willing to participate in this type of program (that is, transnational) in the future. The collected responses were used to test Hypothesis (8):

Each of the targeted transnational programs will be perceived by its students as effective.

This hypothesis was not supported. Only students in one program deemed it effective, and were also willing to participate in this type of program in the future. Although students in another program considered it effective, majority of those students would not enroll in a similar type of program in the future. The third program was regarded as ineffective in both ways. Consequently, the hypothesis was not supported.

Although not effective, all three programs were still regarded worthwhile. A great majority of students in each of the three programs regarded them worthwhile citing the following reasons: the opportunity to obtain a University degree while working full time; flexible program structure; favourable entry requirements; competitive program fees; and, a relatively short duration of the program.

The present face-to-face delivery mode of the programs was found to be preferable to a proposed fully online provision. Students' preference for delivery mode was tested through Hypothesis (9):

Transnational programs based on face-to-face delivery mode will be preferred by students to programs delivered fully online.

This hypothesis was confirmed. Students strongly opposed fully online provision of transnational programs, and were adamant about the importance of face-to-face contact with both lecturers and fellow students. They cited face-to-face communication as superior in offering instant feedback, affording easier communication with fellow students and instructors, being better suited to the resolution of study problems, and giving better motivation to study. Some students opined that face-to-face communication was more suitable for Hong Kong students because of Hong Kong people's traditional attitudes towards education. The Internet was acknowledged as a useful means for provision of course material and an additional way for communication with instructors and fellow students.

5.3.2. Development and validation of a multidimensional model for transnational computing education programs

The conceptual model for transnational education programs that I developed in this study was applied for validation to three transnational computing programs. The aims of the validation were to determine: (1) how the multiple dimensions of the model were apparent in those programs; (2) if some of the individual attributes within each dimension were more important to students than others; and (3), if any additional attributes or dimensions need to be incorporated in the model.

All the attributes comprising the dimensions of the model were acknowledged by the evaluating students as important to the effectiveness of transnational programs; this was confirmed by the conclusion to Hypothesis (1):

Critical success attributes (of effective distance education programs) in each dimension will be evident in each targeted transnational program.

This hypothesis was supported. The evaluation confirmed the inclusion of all the attributes in the existing dimensions; every attribute was acknowledged as at least 'somewhat important'.

In every dimension of the model, some attributes were deemed as more important to the effectiveness of a program than others; this was evidenced by the conclusion to Hypothesis (2):

Some attributes will be regarded as more important to the success of transnational programs than others.

This hypothesis was confirmed. The transnational students, irrespective of their program, agreed on the attributes that they considered most important to the effectiveness of transnational programs; the extent of agreement was substantial. As a consequence of the ranking of attributes, the model was refined to order attributes within dimensions in terms of their perceived importance, and exclude attributes uniformly considered as least important.

Additional attributes were identified throughout the course of model validation; their discovery was aided by Hypothesis (3):

Additional attributes, not included in the current dimensional model, will be identified as critical to the effectiveness of transnational programs.

This hypothesis was supported. Three additional attributes were identified as critical to program effectiveness: program cost, program duration, and extent of recognition for prior qualifications. Consequently, the model was refined through the introduction of a new dimension, *Pre-enrolment considerations*, to accommodate the newly identified attributes.

Students had the same expectations with respect to University instructors and local instructors, as evidenced by the conclusion to Hypothesis (4):

In each of the targeted programs, attributes regarded as important with respect to University instructor, will be also regarded as important with respect to local instructor.

This hypothesis was also supported. Students in each of the evaluated programs nominated the same critical success attributes for University instructors and local instructors. Instructor attributes perceived as the most influential include appreciation of course requirements and students' needs, and preparedness and organisation.

5.4. CONTRIBUTIONS OF MY STUDY

My study offers contributions in three areas: (1) transnational education in general; (2) effectiveness of transnational education programs; and, (3) design, development, and review of transnational programs. First, in terms of transnational education, this study supports the widely held notion (Chen, 1997; Debowski, 2003; Emil, 2001; Evans & Tregenza, 2002; Herrmann et al., 2001; Knipe, 2002; Marold et al., 2000; Marold & Haga, 2004; Tomasic, 2002; Ziguras, 2000; Ziguras, 2002) that face-to-face interaction is a noteworthy factor in effective transnational learning. This study also contributes to the debate on the reportedly increasing economic rationale of transnational education (De Vita & Case, 2003; Feast & Bretag, 2005; Marginson, 2004a, McBurnie & Ziguras, 2003). While institutions are said to be *motivated as much by profits as by teaching and learning objectives* (Feast & Bretag, 2005, p.64), this study suggests that the economic rationale may have an effect on students; they seem to regard competitive program fees, relatively short program duration, and recognition of prior qualifications resulting in generous subject exemptions as just as important as educational objectives.

Second, my study contributes in three ways towards knowledge about effectiveness of transnational education programs: (1), it responds to the calls for research into quality and effectiveness of distance education programs including transnational programs (Bates, 2000; Marginson, 2002; Moore & Kearsley, 2005; Nasseh, 1997); (2), it addresses the need for a holistic approach to the issue of effectiveness (Dhanarajan, 1999; Phipps & Merisotis, 1999; Wenger, 1998); and (3), it brings in the much needed and called for student perspective into the debate (Carter, 2001; Chapman & Pyvis, 2005; Chapman & Pyvis, 2006). The model for effective transnational programs that I reported in this study was developed with the notion in mind that as the ultimate clients of an education program, students should participate in defining what constitutes its effectiveness. The model offers an insight into learners' perceptions of their educational experience, by providing a detailed account of the wide range of factors that might have influence on those perceptions. Given the information contained herein, it is evident that to improve and sustain transnational programs in the future, it is essential for universities to gain an understanding of the learners' perspective: an understanding that transcends attendance records and academic achievements.

Third, in terms of assisting in the design, development, and review of transnational programs, this study could be pertinent to staff involved in those programs, as well as to university administrators. For staff, it could provide a platform for reflection on what is 'right' or 'wrong' with a program, and which practices are effective or non-effective. Understanding of how the learning experience discourages or frustrates learners might enable staff to consider and implement constructive changes. For instance, the perceived importance of timely feedback on assignments, and the perceived failure of the programs to deliver it, identifies one aspect of the programs evaluated in this study that calls for attention.

For university administrators, this study could provide assistance in reviewing the quality and consistency of their transnational offerings. For instance, it has been argued that transnational programs should be of equivalent standard to the same programs offered by the university at home (Biggs, 2001; Hyam, 2003; Van Damme, 2001), and various university quality policies include that requirement. Yet, this study revealed significant differences between perceived performance of university and local lecturers in the evaluated programs, which might undermine the requirement of equivalent program standard; this is one issue for university administrators to consider. Likewise, university policies and, in some instances, dedicated university units aim to ensure that all transnational education programs offered under the university are delivering a sound education consistent and compliant with well defined standards (Hentea et al., 2003). Yet, this study revealed significant differences between perceived satisfaction with two programs offered by the same university, potentially challenging the requirement of intra-institutional consistency of transnational programs; this is another issue for the university administrators to address.

5.5. CONSTRAINTS AND LIMITATIONS

As with any research study, there is a possibility of flaws in design, data, and interpretation. In my study, one consideration that needs to be taken into account is the fact that the study was designed to investigate Australian transnational education that is, one including face-to-face delivery. Consequently, the generalisability of the study results with respect to other types of transnational education would be limited.

Regarding the applicability of the results of this study to Australian transnational education, the sampling of data from programs offered only in Hong Kong does not lend itself to cross-validation of the model against different educational contexts; the validation is constrained by the dependence on the milieu in which the research was conducted, providing only limited generalisability of the model with respect to programs offered in other countries.

5.6. RECOMMENDATIONS FOR FURTHER RESEARCH

Research into effectiveness of transnational education is still in its initial stages. This study is distinctive because it contributes to the overall body of knowledge related to transnational education, to studies of higher education, and to research of effectiveness in a developing area of transnational education. However, further studies related to these three areas need to be continued.

A larger multinational sample would be desirable to expand upon the generalisability of what I have reported in this initial development and validation of the multidimensional model for transnational programs. A study of transnational programs offered by universities from countries other than Australia, and programs offered in destinations other than Hong Kong, would be advantageous by introducing larger variation in student perceptions; this could also assist in determining any cultural influences.

In addition, a study differentiating between undergraduate and postgraduate programs might illuminate the differences in the perceptions of students seeking their first degree as opposed to students seeking further university qualifications. There are likely to be differences between these two types of students and what they consider to be important attributes of transnational programs.

Further research is needed to confirm that the multiple dimensions of the model are not a collection of separate entities, but parts of an integrated system. The interactions between the dimensions and the extent to which they impact on each other will have to be examined. This could assist distance education providers planning new programs, or considering changes to existing programs, in determining the impact of their decisions.

Likewise, an additional study could be carried out to explore any associations between students' satisfaction with various aspects of transnational programs and their perceptions of the importance of those aspects to program effectiveness. For instance, this study found that students in all evaluated programs were most dissatisfied with the time taken to mark their assignments and provide feedback. At the same time, students perceived timely feedback on assignments and project as the most important aspect of the *Interaction* dimension; did they regard it important because it was lacking?

Finally, the validation of the model was only conducted on data obtained from transnational students. An expanded study could be conducted using the same analyses on data obtained from University and local instructors. Such a study would enable examination of the similarities and differences in perceptions of program effectiveness between the various participants of the transnational context.

5.7. CONCLUDING REMARKS

Research on the effectiveness of transnational education faces the dilemma that the educational context is not homogenous, as it involves different types of educational providers, students, and partner institutions across many countries and, it includes a variety of program delivery models. In addition, the educational context is constantly evolving due to the introduction of new technologies and, resulting from it, the introduction of new ways of teaching and learning. My study provides support for investigating effectiveness of transnational programs in that, irrespective of how the educational context may change in the future, the fundamental factors that impact learning and success have been identified by 'insiders and experts': the transnational students themselves.

REFERENCES

Adam, S. (2001). Transnational Education Project: Report and Recommendations. Confederation of European Union Rectors' Conferences, University of Westminster. Retrieved May, 2005 from http://www.crue.org/espaeuro/transnational_education_project.pdf

Allen, M., Bourhis, J., Burrell, N., & Mabry, E. (2002). Comparing student satisfaction with distance education to traditional classrooms in higher education: A meta-analysis. *The American Journal of Distance Education, 16*, 83-97.

Allport, C. (2000). Thinking globally, acting locally. Lifelong learning and the implications for university staff. *Journal of Higher Education Policy and Management, 22*(1), 37-46.

Aslanian, C. (2001). *Adult students today.* The College Board: New York. Cited in Paradigm, *13*(3). Retrieved March, 2006 from http://www.mercyhurst.edu/graduate/paradigm-newsletter-pdf/fall2001.pdf

Australian Education International (2002). *Comparative Costs of Higher Education Courses for International Students in Australia, New Zealand, the United Kingdom, Canada and the United States.* Department of Education, Science and Training: Canberra.

AVCC (Australian Vice Chancellors' Committee) (2005). Report, January 2005. Retrieved March, 2006 from http://www.avcc.edu.au/documents/publications/stats/International.pdf

Bajtelsmit, J.W. (1998). *Predicting distance learning dropouts: testing a conceptual model of attrition in distance education.* Bryn Mawr, PA: American College.

Bates, T. (1995). *Technology: Open learning and distance education.* New York: Routledge.

Bates, T. (2000). Distance education in dual mode higher education institutions: Challenges and changes. Retrieved March, 2006 from http://bates.cstudies.ubc.ca/papers/challengesandchanges.html

Bates, A.W., & de los Santos, J.G.E. (1997). Crossing boundaries: Making global distance education a reality. *Journal of Distance Education, 12*(1/2), 49-66.

Beaudoin, M. (1990). The instructors changing role in distance education. *The American Journal of Distance Education, 4*(2), 21-29.

Beard, L.A., & Harper, C. (2002). Student perceptions of online versus campus instruction. *Education, 122*, 658-663.

Belanger, F., & Jordan, D. H. (2000). *Evaluation and implementation of distance learning: Technologies, tools, and techniques.* Hershey, PA: Idea Group.

Ben-Jacob, M.G. (1998). *Teaching mathematics, science and technology on the Internet: A workshop.* Proceedings of the annual conference on distance teaching & learning (ERIC Document Reproduction Service No. ED422842).

Bernt, F.L., & Bugbee, A.C. (1993). Study practices and attitudes related to academic success in a distance learning programme. *Distance Education, 14*(1), 97-112.

Biggs, J. (2001). The reflective institution: assuring and enhancing the quality of teaching and learning. *Higher Education, 41*(3), 221-238.

Billings, D.M. (1988). A conceptual model of correspondence course completion. *The American Journal of Distance Education, 2*(2), 23-35.

Biner, P.M. (1993). The development of an instrument to measure student attitudes toward televised courses. *The American Journal of Distance Education, 7*(1), 62-70.

Biner, P.M., Dean, R.S., & Mellinger, A.E. (1994). Factors underlying distance learner satisfaction with televised college-level courses. *The American Journal of Distance Education, 8*(1), 60-71.

Bjarnason, S. (2005). MBA in higher education management. Seminar presentation. *Observatory on Higher Borderless Education*. Retrieved March, 2006 from http://www.obhe.ac.uk/resources/speeches/mba_higher_education.pdf

Blumenstyk, G. (1999). The marketing intensifies in distance learning. *Chronicle of Higher Education, 45*(31), 27-30.

Brown, B.M. (1998). Digital classrooms: Some myths about developing new educational programs using the internet. *T H E Journal (Technological Horizons in Education)*, Dec, 1-5. Retrieved August 2005 from http://thejournal.com/articles/14064

Brown, R., & Dale, E. (1989*). Overseas students: Educational opportunity and challenge*. Curtin, ACT: The Australian College of Education.

Buchanan, E.A. (2000). Going the extra mile: Serving distance education students with resources and services. *Syllabus: New directions in education technology, 13*(9), 44-47.

Burge, E.J. (1994). Learning in computer conferenced contexts: The learners' perspective. *Journal of Distance Education, 9*(1), 19-43.

Capper, J. (1999). Distance education in uncertain times. In R.Carr, O.J.Jegede, T.M.Wong & K.S.Yuen (Eds.), *The Asian Distance Learner* (pp.23-32). Hong Kong: Open University of Hong Kong Press.

Carnevale, A.P. (1999). A college degree is the key. *CrossTalk, 7*(3), 10-11.

Carr, S. (2000). As distance education comes of age, the challenge is keeping the students. *The Chronicle of Higher Education, 46*(23), A39-A41.

Carter, A. (2001). Interactive distance education: Implications for the adult learner. *International Journal of Instructional Media, 28*(3), 249-261.

Cashion, J., & Palmieri, P. (2002). *The secret is the teacher: The learner's view of online learning.* Leabrook, South Australia: Australian National Training Authority. Retrieved December, 2004 from http://www.ncver.edu.au/publications/906.html

Cavanaugh, C.S. (2001). The effectiveness of interactive distance education technologies in K-12 learning: A meta-analysis. *International Journal of Educational Telecommunications, 7*(1), 73-88.

Cetron, M.J., & Davies, O. (2005). Trends shaping the future: Technological, workplace, management, and institutional trends. *The Futurist, 39*(3), 37-50.

Chapman, A., & Pyvis, D. (2005). Identity and social practice in higher education: student experiences of postgraduate courses delivered 'offshore' in Singapore and Hong Kong by an Australian university. *International Journal of Educational Development, 25*, 39-52.

Chapman, A., & Pyvis, D. (2006). Quality, identity and practice in offshore university programmes: Issues in the internationalization of Australian higher education. *Teaching in Higher Education, 11*(2), 233-245.

Charp, S. (1997). Strategies for bridging distances. *THE Journal (Technological Horizons in Education), 24*(9), 6-8.

Chen, L. (1997). Distance delivery systems in terms of pedagogical considerations: A revolution. *Educational Technology, 37*(4), 34-37.

Chickering, A.W., & Ehrmann, S.C. (1996). Implementing the seven principles: technology as lever. *AAHE Bulletin, 49*(2), 3-6. Retrieved March, 2003 from http://www.tltgroup.org/programs/seven.html

Chickering, A., & Gamson, Z. (1987). Seven principles of good practice in undergraduate education. *AAHE Bulletin, 39*(7), 3-6.

Christensen, E. W., Anakwe, U. P. & Kessler, E. H. (2001). Receptivity to distance learning: The effect of technology, reputation, constraints, and learning preferences. *Journal of Research on Computing in Education, 33*(3), 263-279.

Chute, A.G., Thompson, M.M., & Hancock, B.W. (1999). *The McGraw-Hill Handbook of Distance Learning* (pp.162-194). New York: McGraw-Hill.

Chyung, Y., Winiecki, D.J., & Fenner, J.A. (1998). *Evaluation of effective interventions to solve the dropout problem in adult distance education.* Retrieved March, 2005 from http://coen.boisestate.edu/ychyung/edmedia.htm

Clark, R.E., & Craig T.G. (1992). Research and theory on multi-media learning effects. In M. Giardina (Ed.), *Interactive multimedia learning environments: Human factors and technical considerations on design issues* (pp. 19-30). New York: Springer-Verlag.

Confederation of European Union Rectors' Conferences (2001). Transnational Education Project: Report and Recommendations. *Conference on Transnational Education,* Malmö, Sweden. Retrieved November, 2004 from http://www.unesco.org/education/studyingabroad/highlights/global_forum/reference/tne.doc

Cornell, R., & Martin, B.L. (1997). The role of motivation in Web-based instruction. In B.H. Kahn (Ed.), *Web-based instruction,* (pp. 93-100). Englewood Cliff, NJ: Educational Technology Publications.

Cunningham, S., Ryan, Y., Stedman, L., Tapsall, S., Bagdon, K., Flew, T., & Coaldrake, P. (2000). *The Business of Borderless Education* (pp. 18-23). Canberra: DETYA.

Daniel, J., & Marquis, C. (1983). Independence and interaction: Getting the mix right. *Teaching at a distance, 15*, 29-44.

Dasher-Alston, R.M., & Patton, G.W. (1998). Evaluation criteria for distance learning. *Planning for Higher Education, 27*, 11-17.

Davis, D., & Meares, D. (Eds) (2001). *Transnational education: Australia online – critical factors for success*. Sydney: IDP Education Australia.

Debowski, S. (2003). Lost in internationalised space: The challenge of sustaining academics teaching offshore. *17th IDP Australian International Education Conference, Securing the future for international education*. Melbourne, Australia. Retrieved August, 2004 from http://www.idp.com/17aiecpapers/

Denning, P., Comer, D.E., Gries, D., Mulder, M.C., Tucker, A., Turner, A.J., & Young, P.R. (1989). Computing as a discipline. *Communications of the ACM, 32*(1), 9-23.

DEST (Department of Education, Science and Training) (2005). A national quality strategy for Australian transnational education and training: A discussion paper. Retrieved October, 2005 from http://aei.dest.gov.au/AEI/GovernmentActivities/QAAustralianEducationAndTrainingSystem/QualStrat_pdf.pdf

De Vita, G., & Case, P. (2003). Rethinking the internationalisation agenda in UK higher education. *Journal of Further and Higher Education, 27*(4), 383-398.

Dhanarajan, G. (1999). Foreword. In K. Harry (Ed.), *Higher education through open and distance learning* (pp. xiii-xiv). London: Routledge.

Dhanarajan, G., & Timmers, S. (1992). Transfer and adaptation of self-instructional materials: Issues for consideration. *Open Learning, 7*(1), 3-11.

Dillon, C.L., & Gunawardena, C.N. (1995). A framework for the evaluation of telecommunication-based distance education. In D. Sewart (Ed.), *One world, many voices: Quality in open and distance learning* (pp. 348–351). Birmingham, England: The Open University.

Dillon, C.L., & Walsh, S.M. (1992). Faculty: The neglected resource in distance education. *The American Journal of Distance Education, 6*(3), 5-21.

Doucette, D. (1994). Transforming teaching and learning using information technology. *Community College Journal, 65*(2), 18-24.

Duffy, T. M., & Kirkley, J. R. (2004). Learning theory and pedagogy applied in distance learning: The case of Cardean University. In T.M. Duffy & J.R. Kirkley (Eds.), *Learner-centered theory and practice in distance education*. Mahwah, NJ: Lawrence Erlbaum Associates.

Dunn, S. (2000). The virtualizing of education. *The Futurist, 34*(2), 34-38.

Dupin-Bryant, P. (2004). Variables related to interactive television teaching style: In search of learner-centered teaching styles. *International Journal of Instructional Technology and Distance Learning, 1*(4), 3-14.

Dzakiria, H. (2003). Does technology promote interaction in distance learning? Distance learners' perspective, *Malaysian Journal of Educational Technology, 3*(1), 7-20.

Egan, M. W., Sebastian, J., & Welch, M. (1991). Effective television teaching: Perceptions of those who count most …distance learners. *Proceedings of the Rural Education Symposium.* Nashville, TN. (ERIC Document Reproduction Service No. ED373708)

Ehrmann, S. (2005). The history of the Flashlight Program. *Assessment Update, 9*(4), 10-11. Retrieved September, 2005 from http://www.tltgroup.org/programs/elephant.html

Emil, B. (2001). Distance learning, access, and opportunity: Equality and e-quality. *Metropolitan Universities, 12*(1), 19.

Evans, T., & Tregenza, K. (2002). Academics' experiences of teaching Australian 'non-local' courses in Hong Kong. Paper presented at the *Australian Association for Research in Education Conference, Crossing borders: New frontiers for educational research.* Brisbane, Australia. Retrieved February, 2006 from http://www.aare.edu.au/02pap/eva02510.htm

Fahy, P. J., & Archer, L. M. (1999). On-line learning: How accessible? *Open Praxis, 1,* 15-18.

Feast, V., & Bretag, T. (2005). Responding to crisis in transnational education: new challenges for higher education. *Higher Education Research and Development, 24*(1), 63-78.

Fenn, D. (1999). Corporate universities for small companies. *Inc.Online,* February. Retrieved August, 2003 from http://www.inc.com/magazine/19990201/730.html

Firestone, W.A. (1987). Meaning in method: The rhetoric of quantitative and qualitative research. *Educational Researcher, 16*(7), 16-21.

Fox, J. (1998). Distance education: Is it good enough? *The University Concourse, 3*(4), 3-5.

Frantz, G., & King, J. W. (2000). The distance education learning systems model (DEL). *Educational Technology, 40*(3), 33-40.

Fraser, S., & Deane, E. (1998). *Doers and thinkers: An investigation of the use of open-learning strategies to develop life-long learning competencies in undergraduate science students* (pp. 8-9). University of Western Sydney, Nepean: Evaluations and Investigations Programme, Higher Education Division, DEETYA.

Freeman, M.A., & Capper, J.M. (1999). Educational innovation: Hype, heresies and hopes. *ALN Magazine, 3*(2). Retrieved March, 2005 from http://www.sloan-c.org/publications/magazine/v3n2/freeman.asp

Frew, E.A., & Weber, K. (1995). Towards a higher retention rate among distance learners, *Open Learning: the Journal of Open and Distance Learning, 10*(2), 62-65.

Fulford, C.P., & Zhang, S. (1993). Perceptions of interaction: The critical predictor in distance education. *The American Journal of Distance Education, 7*(3), 8-21.

Galante, D. (1997). Distance learning in the mathematics classroom: Student satisfaction and the use of interactive television. Retrieved January, 2003 from http://www.coe.ilstu.edu/phklass/eaf509/paper/pap/galante.htm

Gallagher, M. (2001). E-learning in Australia; universities and the new distance education. 7th *OECD/Japan seminar E-learning in post-secondary education*, Tokyo. Retrieved November, 2004 from http://www.oecd.org/dataoecd/16/52/1854142.pdf

Gallagher, P.A., & McCormick, K. (1999). Student satisfaction with two-way interactive distance learning for delivery of early childhood special education coursework. *Journal of Special Education Technology, 14*(1), 32-47.

Garland, M.R. (1993). Student perceptions of the situational, institutional, dispositional and epistemological barriers to persistence. *Distance Education, 14*(2), 181-198.

Garrison, D.R., & Shale, D. (1987). Mapping the boundaries of distance education: Problems in defining the field. *The American Journal of Distance Education, 1*(1), 7-13.

GATE (Global Alliance for Transnational Education) (2000). *Demand for transnational education in the Asia Pacific*, Washington: Global Alliance for Transnational Education.

GDNET (Global Distance Education Net) (2005). Management: Governance and structure. Online resource. Retrieved November, 2005 from http://gdenet.idln.or.id/

Gibbs, G., & Simpson, C. (2004). *Does your assessment support your students' learning?* Centre for Higher Education Practice, Open University. Retrieved July 2005, from http://www.open.ac.uk/science/fdtl/documents/lit-review.pdf

Gibson, C.C. (1998). In retrospect. In C.C. Gibson (Ed.). *Distance learners in higher education* (pp. 139-143). Madison, Wisconsin: Atwood Pub.

Gibson, C. C. (2003). Learners and learning: The need for theory. In M. G. Moore & W. G. Anderson (Eds.), *Handbook of distance education*. Mahwah, NJ: Lawrence Erlbaum Associates.

Gilbert, S. (2001). *How to be a successful online student.* New York: McGraw-Hill.

Goodfellow, R., Lea, M., Gonzalez, F., & Mason, R. (2001). Opportunity and e-quality: Intercultural and linguistic issues in global online learning. *Distance Education, 22*(1), 65-84.

Granger, D., & Benke, M. (1998). Supporting learners at a distance from inquiry through completion. In C.C. Gibson (Ed.). *Distance learners in higher education* (pp. 127-137). Madison, Wisconsin: Atwood Pub.

Granger, D., & Bowman, M. (2003). Constructing knowledge at a distance: The learner context. In M. G. Moore & W. G. Anderson (Eds.), *Handbook of distance education*. Mahwah, NJ: Lawrence Erlbaum Associates.

Greenbaum, T.L. (1998). *The handbook of focus group research*, (2nd Ed.). Thousand Oaks, CA: Sage Publications.

Greenberg, G. (1998). Distance education technologies: Best practices for K-12 settings. *IEEE Technology and Society Magazine*, Winter, 36-40.

Gubernick, L., & Ebeling, A. (1997). I got my degree through e-mail. *Forbes, 159*(12), 84-86.

Gunawardena, C.N., & McIsaac, M.S. (2005). Distance education. *Association for Educational Communications and Technology*, Chapter 14, 355-395. Retrieved September, 2005 from http://www.aect.org/edtech/14.pdf

Gunawardena, C.N., & Zittle, F.J. (1997). Social presence as a predictor of satisfaction within a computer-mediated conferencing environment. *The American Journal of Distance Education, 11*(3), 8-26.

Gururajan, V. (2002). Knowledge management a new game in higher education: A discussion paper on the new trends of technology influencing the higher education landscape. In *Focusing on the Student*. Proceedings of the 11th Annual Teaching Learning Forum, 5-6 February 2002. Perth: Edith Cowan University. Retrieved December, 2004 from http://lsn.curtin.edu.au/tlf/tlf2002/abstracts/gururajan-abs.html

Guskin, A.E. (1994). Reducing student costs & enhancing student learning. Part II: Restructuring the role of faculty. *Change, 26*(5), 16-25.

Hall, J. (1995). The convergence of means. *Educom Review, 30*(4), 42-45. Retrieved September, 2003 from http://www.educause.edu/pub/er/review/reviewArticles/30442.html

Hamza, M.K., & Alhalabi, B. (1999). Technology and education: Between chaos and order. *First Monday, 4*(3). Online journal. Retrieved November, 2003 from http://www.firstmonday.dk/issues/issue4_3/hamza/

Hara, N., & Kling, R. (1999). Students' frustrations with a web-based distance education course. *First Monday, 4*(12). Retrieved May, 2003 from http://www.firstmonday.org/issues/issue4_12/hara/index.html

Hardy D.W., & Boaz, M.H. (1997). Learner development: Beyond the technology. In T.E. Cyrs (Ed.), *Teaching and learning at a distance: What it takes to effectively design, deliver, and evaluate programs* (pp. 41-48). San Francisco: Jossey-Bass.

Harman, G. (2004). New directions in internationalising higher education: Australia's development as an exporter of higher education services. *Higher Education Policy, 17*(1), 101–120.

Heinich, R., Molenda, M., Russell, J., & Smaldino, S. (1996). *Educational media and technologies for learning*. Columbus, OH: Merrill/Prentice Hall.

Hentea, M., Shea, M.J., & Pennington, L. (2003). A perspective on fulfilling the expectations of distance education. *In Proceedings of the 4th Conference on information technology education (CITC4 2003)*, 160-167. Lafayette, Indiana, USA, October 16-18, 2003. ACM Press, New York.

Herrmann, A., Downie, J., & O'Connell, B. (2001). Assessing and evaluating student contribution to electronic discussions. *Australian Electronic Journal of Nursing Education, 7*(1). Retrieved October, 2005 from http://www.scu.edu.au/schools/nhcp/aejne/archive/vol7-1/refereed/oconnell.html

Hillman, D.C., Willis, D.J., & Gunawardena, C.N. (1994). Learner-interface interaction in distance education: An extension of contemporary models and strategies for practitioners. *The American Journal of Distance Education, 8*(2), 30-42.

Hiltz, S.R., & Wellman, B. (1997). A synchronous learning network as a virtual classroom. *Communications of the ACM, 40*(9), 44-49.

Holifield, D., & Thomas, N. (1999). Training partnership: Is it a life-long learning partnership and who benefits? *Global Journal of Engineering Education, 3*(3), 195-198. Retrieved March, 2006 from http://eng.monash.edu.au/uicee/gjee/vol3no3/holifield1.pdf

Holmberg, B. (1995). *Theory and practice of distance education* (2nd Ed.). London: Routledge.

Holmberg, B., & Bakshi, T.S. (1982). Laboratory work in distance education. *Distance Education, 3*(2), 198-206.

Hong, K.S. (2002). Relationships between students; and instructional variables with satisfaction and learning from Web-based course. *The Internet and Higher Education, 5*(3), 267-281.

Hong Kong Government (1996). *Non-local Higher and Professional Education (Regulation) Ordinance.*

Howell, B., & Jayaratna, N. (2000). Demonstration of how soft systems methodology can be used to structure the issues associated with distance learning activities. In Orange, G. & Hobbs, D. (Eds.), *International perspectives on tele-education and virtual learning environments* (pp. 91-108). Aldershot, England: Ashgate Publishing Ltd.

Howell, S.L., Williams, P.B., & Lindsay, N.K. (2004). Thirty-two trends affecting distance education: An informed foundation for strategic planning. *Online Journal of Distance Learning Administration, 6*(3). Retrieved March, 2006 from http://www.emich.edu/cfid/PDFs/32Trends.pdf

Huang, F. (2003). Transnational higher education: A perspective from China. *Higher Education Research and Development, 22*(2), 193-203.

Huch, M. (1999). Where does the information superhighway go? *Nursing Science Quarterly, 12*(3), 215-220.

Hyam, L. (2003). Australian higher education and quality: International issues, challenges and opportunities. Keynote address. *Proceedings of the Australian Universities Quality Forum 2003.* AUQA occasional publication. Retrieved October, 2005 from http://www.auqa.edu.au/auqf/2003/program/papers/Hyam.pdf

IDP Education Australia (2000). *Transnational education providers, partners and policy: Challenges for Australian institutions offshore.* D. Davis, A. Olsen & A. Böhm (Eds.). IDP: Canberra.

IDP Education Australia (2002). *The global student mobility 2025: Forecasts of the global demand for international higher education.* Report. IDP: Canberra.

IDP Education Australia (2004). *International students in Australian universities.* Report, semester 2, 2004. IDP: Canberra. Retrieved March, 2006 from http://www.idp.com/research/fastfacts/Semester%20Two%202004%20-%20Key%20Outcomes_Web.pdf

Inman, E., & Kerwin, M. (1999). Instructor and student attitudes toward distance learning. *Community College Journal of Research & Practice, 23*(6), 581-592

Irons, L., Jung, D., & Keel, R. (2002). Interactivity in distance learning: The digital divide and student satisfaction. *Educational Technology & Society, 5*(3). Retrieved May, 2004 from http://ifets.ieee.org/periodical/vol_3_2002/jung.html

Jonassen, D.H. (1985). Interactive lesson designs: A taxonomy. *Educational Technology Magazine, 25*(6), 7-17.

Jones, D. (1996). Computing by distance education. *ACM SIGCSE/SIGCUE Conference on Integrating Technology into Computer Science Education,* Barcelona, June 1996. Retrieved June, 2005 from http://cq-pan.cqu.edu.au/david-jones/Publications/Papers_and_Books/96acm/

Jones, G.R. (2001). Bridging the challenges of transnational education and accreditation. *Higher Education in Europe,* 26(1), 107-116.

Jones, G.R. (2002). Opening remarks. *Global Alliance for Transnational Education (GATE) Conference.* Paris: France, 18-20 September, 2002. Retrieved November 2002, from http://www.edugate.org/conferences/powerpoints/Jones/Jones%20Speech.pdf

Jung, I., Choi, S., Lim, C., & Leem, J. (2002). Effects of different types of interaction on learning achievement, satisfaction and participation in Web-based instruction. *Innovations in Education and Teaching International, 39*(2), 153-162.

Keast, D.A. (1997). Toward an effective model for implementing distance education programs. *The American Journal of Distance Education, 11*(2), 39-55.

Keegan, D. (1996). *The foundations of distance education* (3rd Ed.). London: Routledge.

Kember, D. (1982). External science courses: The practicals problem. *Distance Education, 3*(2), 207-225.

Kember, D. (1995). *Open learning for adults: A model of student progress.* Englewood Cliffs. NJ: Educational Technology Publications.

Kember, D. (1999). The learning experience of Asian students: A challenge to widely held beliefs. In R.Carr, O.J.Jegede, T.M.Wong, & K.S.Yuen (Eds.), *The Asian Distance Learner* (pp.82-99). Hong Kong: Open University of Hong Kong Press.

Kenny, A. (2002). Online learning: Enhancing nurse education? *Journal of Advanced Nursing, 38*(2), 127-135.

Khoo, C. S., & Idrus, R.M. (2004). A study of quality assurance practices in the Universiti Sains Malaysia (USM), Malaysia. *Turkish Online Journal of Distance Education*, *5*(1), 1-7. Retrieved March 2004 from http://tojde.anadolu.edu.tr/tojde13/articles/idrus.html

King, E. (1999). Education revised for a world in transformation. *Comparative Education*, *35*(2), 109-117.

Kirkup, G., & Jones, A. (1996). New technologies for open learning: The superhighway to the learning society? In P. Raggatt, R. Edwards, & N. Small (Eds.), *Adult learners, education and training 2: The learning society – challenges and trends* (pp.272-291). London: Routledge.

Kirkwood, A. (1998). New media mania: Can information and communication technologies enhance the quality of open and distance learning? *Distance Education*, *19*(2), 228-241.

Kiser, K. (2002). Is blended best? *E-Learning*, *3*(6), 10.

Knight, J. (2004). Internationalism remodeled: Definition, approaches and rationales. *Journal of Studies in International Education*, *8*(1), 5-31.

Knipe, D. (2002). The quality of teaching and learning via videoconferencing. *British Journal of Educational Technology*, *33*(3), 301-311.

Knott, T.D. (1992). Determining societal needs for distance education in tomorrow's global village. *Educational Media International*, *29*(3), 162-64.

Langford, D., R. & Hardin, S. (1999). Distance learning: Issues emerging as the paradigm shifts. *Nursing Science Quarterly*, *12*(3), 191-196.

Leach, K., & Walker, S. (2000). Internet-based distance education: Barriers, models and new research. In G. Davies & C. Owen (Eds.) *WebNet 2000 World Conference on the WWW and Internet Proceedings*, (pp.903-905). Association for the Advancement of Computers in Education: Charlottesville, VA. Retrieved May, 2005 from http://www.itouch.net/~swalker/smec/internet_based_distance_education.pdf

Leask, B. (2004). Transnational education and intercultural learning: Reconstructing the offshore teaching team to enhance internationalization. *Proceedings of the Australian Universities Quality Forum 2004* (pp. 144-149). Retrieved October, 2005 from http://www.auqa.edu.au/auqf/2004/proceedings/AUQF2004_Proceedings.pdf

Le Grew, D. (1995). Global knowledge: Superhighway or super gridlock. *Applications of media and technology in higher education*. Chiba, Japan: National Institute of Multimedia Education.

Lewis, L., Farris, E., & Alexander, D. (1997). *Distance education in higher education*. Statistical Analysis Report (Report No. NCES-98-062). Rockville, MD: Westat, Inc. (ERIC Document Reproduction No. 413 829).

Lewis, J.H., & Romiszowski, A. (1996). Networking and the learning organization: Networking issues and scenarios for the 21st century. *Journal of Instructional Science and Technology*, *1*(4)

[Online]. Retrieved May, 2003 from http://www.usq.edu.au/electpub/e-jist/docs/old/vol1no4/article1.htm

Lim, C.K. (2001). Computer self-efficacy, academic self-concept and other predictors of satisfaction and future participation of adult learners. *American Journal of Distance Education*, *15*(2), 41-51.

Ljoså, E. (1992). Distance education in a modern society. *Open Learning*, *7*(2), 23-30.

Lockee, B., Burton, J., & Cross, L. (1999). No comparison: Distance education finds a new use for "no significant difference." *Educational Technology, Research and Development, 47*(3), 33-43.

Low, B. (1998). Planning and implementing distance learning education: An interaction exchange and relationship approach. Sydney: Nepean, University of Western Sydney.

Macdonald, H.I. (2000). Plenary address. *11th general conference: Universities as gateway to the future*, Plenary Panel II, Durban, South Africa. Retrieved August, 2004 from http://www.unesco.org/iau/conferences/durban/rtf/confdurban31.rtf

Machado dos Santos, S.M. (2002). Regulation and quality assurance in transnational education. *Tertiary Education and Management*, *8*(2), 97-112.

Machtmes, K., & Asher, J.W. (2000). A meta-analysis of the effectiveness of telecourses in distance education. *The American Journal of Distance Education, 14*(1), 27-46

MacKenzie, O., & Christensen, E. (Eds). (1971). *The changing world of correspondence study: International readings*. University Park, PA: Pennsylwania State University Press.

Mak, S. (1999). An interactive multimedia learning on demand system. *Fifth Australian World Wide Web Conference*, Southern Cross University, Lismore, Australia. Retrieved January, 2006 from http://ausweb.scu.edu.au/aw99/papers/mak1/paper.html

Marginson, S. (2002). The phenomenal rise of international degrees Down Under. *Change, 34*(3), 34-43. Retrieved September, 2005 from http://www.findarticles.com/p/articles/mi_m1254/is_3_34/ai_85465152

Marginson, S. (2004a). National and global competition in higher education. *The Australian Educational Researcher, 31*(2), 1-28.

Marginson, S. (2004b). Don't leave me hanging on the Anglophone: The potential for online distance higher education in the Asia-Pacific region. *Higher Education Quarterly, 58*(2/3), 74-113.

Marginson, S. (2004c). National and global competition in higher education: Towards a synthesis (theoretical reflections). Presentation at the *Association for the Study of Higher Education Conference 2004*, Kansas City. Retrieved February, 2006 from: http://www.ashe.ws/paperdepot/2004%20int%20marginson%20national%20and%20global%20competition.pdf

Marold, K., & Haga, W. (2003). The emerging profile of the on-line learner: Relating course performance with pretests, GPA, and other measures of achievement. *IRMA Proceedings*, Idea Group Publishing, 248-251.

Marold, K., & Haga, W. (2004). Measuring online students' ability to apply programming theory: Are Web courses really working? *Journal of International Technology and Information Management*, *13*(1), 13-20.

Marold, K., Larsen, G., & Moreno, A. (2000). *Web-based learning: Is it working? Challenges of information technology management in the 21st Century*. Idea Group Publishing. Hershey, PA, 350-353.

Matthews, D. (1999). The origins of distance education and its use in the United States. *T H E Journal (Technological Horizons in Education)*, *27*(2), 54-61.

Matthews, J. (2002). International education and internationalisation are not the same as globalisation: Emerging issues for secondary schools. *Journal of Studies in International Education*, *6*(4), 369-390.

Mazelan, P.M., Green, D.M., Brannigan, C.R., & Tormey, P.F. (1993). *Student satisfaction and perceptions of quality* (ERIC Document Reproduction Service ED 358 830).

McBurnie, G., & Pollock, A. (1998). Transnational education: An Australian example. *International Higher Education*, *10*, 12-14.

McBurnie, G., & Pollock, A. (2000). Opportunity and risk in transnational education – issue in planning for international campus development: An Australian perspective. *Higher Education in Europe*, *25*(3), 333-343.

McBurnie, G., & Ziguras, C. (2003). Remaking the world in our own image: Australia's effort to liberalise trade in education services. *Australian Journal of Education*, *47*(3), 217-234.

McDonough, J., & McDonough, S. (1997). *Research methods for English language teachers*. London: Arnold.

McElhinney, J., & Nasseh, B. (1999). Technical and pedagogical challenges faced by faculty and students in computer-based distance education in higher education in the United States. *Journal of Educational Technology*, *27*(4) 349-359.

McIsaac, M. S. (1998). Distance learning: The U.S. version. *Performance Improvement Quarterly*, *12*(2), 21-35.

McIsaac, M.S., Blocher, J.M., Mahes, V., & Vrasidas, C. (1999). Student and teacher perceptions of interaction in online computer-mediated communication. *Educational Media International*, *36*(2), 121-131.

McLoughlin, C. (2001). Inclusivity and alignment: Principles of pedagogy, task and assessment design for effective cross cultural online learning. *Distance Education*, *22*(1), 7-29.

McLoughlin, C., Oliver R., & Wood, D. (1999). Pedagogic roles and dynamics in telematics environments. In M. Selinger, & J. Pearson (Eds.), *Telematics in education: Trends and issues* (pp. 32-50). Oxford, U.K.: Elsevier Science Ltd.

Meares, D. (2001). Australia Online. In D. Davis, & D. Meares (Eds.) *Transnational education Australia online, critical factors for success* (pp. 7-20). Sydney: IDP Australia.

Meister, J. (1998). *Corporate universities: Lessons in building a world-class workforce* (2nd Edn.). New York : McGraw Hill.

Merisotis, J., & Phipps, R. (1999). What's the difference? *Change, 31*(3), 13-17. Retrieved in November, 2004 from http://www.findarticles.com/p/articles/mi_m1254/is_3_31/ai_55015324/pg_1

Middlehurst, R. (2003). The developing world of borderless higher education: Markets, providers, quality assurance and qualifications. In *Conference proceedings of the first global forum on international quality assurance, accreditation and the recognition of qualifications.* Paris, UNESCO, 25-39.

Molenda, M., & Harris, P. (2001). Issues and trends in instructional technology. In R.M. Branch and M.A. Fitzgerald (Eds.), *Educational media and technology yearbook* (Vol. 26, pp.3-15). Englewood, CO: Libraries Unlimited, Inc.

Mood, T.A. (1995). *Distance education: An annotated bibliography.* Eglewood, CO: Libraries Unlimited, Inc.

Moore, M.G. (1989). Three types of interaction. Editorial. *The American Journal of Distance Education, 3*(2), 1-6. Retrieved March, 2005 from http://www.ajde.com/Contents/vol3_2.htm#editorial

Moore, M.G. (1990). Recent contribution to the theory of distance education. *Open Learning, 5*(3), 10-15.

Moore, M.G., & Kearsley, G. (2005). *Distance education: a systems view*, 2nd Edition. Toronto, Canada: Wadsworth.

Morgan, C.K., & McKenzie, A.D. (2003). Is enough too much? The dilemma for online distance learner supporters. *International Review of Research in Open and Distance Learning, 4*(1). Retrieved November, 2004 from http://www.irrodl.org/content/v4.1/mckenzie_morgan.html

Morgan, C.K., & Tam, M. (1999). Unravelling the complexities of distance education student attrition. *Distance Education, Journal of the Open and Distance Learning Association of Australia, 20*(1), 96-108.

Murgatroyd, S., & Woudstra, A. (1990). Issues in the management of distance education. In M.G. Moore (Ed.) *Contemporary issues in American distance education* (pp. 44-57). Toronto, ON: Pergamon Press Canada.

Nasseh, B. (1997). A brief history of distance education. Retrieved November, 2004 from http://www.bsu.edu/classes/nasseh/study/research.html

Neal, E. (1999). Distance education. *National Forum: Phi Kappa Phi Journal, 79*(1), 40-43.

Nelson, B. (2002). *Higher education at the crossroads: An overview paper*, Department of Education, Science and Training: Canberra.

Nelson, B. (2003). *Our universities: Backing Australia's future*, Department of Education, Science and Training: Canberra. Retrieved September, 2005 from http://www.backingaustraliasfuture.gov.au/

Norman, K.L. (1998). Collaborative interactions in support of learning: Models, metaphors, and management. In R. Hazemi, S. Hailes, & S. Wilbur (Eds.), *The digital university: Reinventing the academy* (pp. 39-53). New York: Springer-Verlag.

Olesinski, R.L. et al. (1995). *The operating technician's role in video distance learning.* Paper presented at the Instructional Technology SIG, San Francisco, California. (ERIC Document Reproduction Service No. ED 387 123).

Oliver, R. (2000). Creating meaningful contexts for learning in web-based settings. In *Open Learning, 6-8 December 2000, Brisbane Convention & Exhibition Centre, Queensland 2000.* Brisbane: Learning Network, 53-61.

Omoregie, M. (1997). *Distance learning: An effective educational delivery system.* (Information Analysis 1070). (ERIC Document Reproduction Service No. ED 418 683).

Ouyang, J. R., & Fu, P. (1996). Effective graphic design for teaching in distance education. Presented at *SITE 96: International 7th annual conference of the society for information technology and teacher education*, Phoenix/Mesa, AZ, March 12-16, 1996. Retrieved May, 2005 from http://168.144.129.112/Articles/Principles%20of%20Effective%20Graphic%20Design%20For%20Teaching%20In%20Distance%20Education.rtf

Palloff, R.M., & Pratt, K. (1999). *Building learning communities in cyberspace: Effective strategies for the online classroom.* San Francisco: Jossey-Bass Publishers.

Palloff, R.M, & Pratt, K. (2000). *Making the transition: Helping teachers to teach online.* Paper presented at EDUCAUSE: Thinking it through. Nashville,Tennessee. (ERIC Document Reproduction Service No. ED 452 806).

Palloff, R.M., & Pratt, K. (2001). *Lessons learned in the cyberspace classroom: The realities of online teaching.* San Francisco: Jossey-Bass Publishers.

Parker, A. (1997). A distance education how-to manual: Recommendations from the field. *Educational Technology Review, 8,* 7-10.

Parker, A. (1999). Interaction in distance education: The critical conversation. *Educational Technology Review, 12,* 13-17.

Patton, M.Q. (1987). *How to use qualitative methods in evaluation.* Newbury Park, CA: Sage Publications.

Peek, R. (2000). A distance learning reality check. *Information Today, 17*(2), 30.

Perraton, H. (1988). A theory for distance education. In D. Sewart, D. Keegan, & B. Holmberg (Eds.), *Distance education: International perspectives* (pp. 34-45). New York: Routledge.

Peters, O. (1998). *Learning and teaching in distance education: analyses and interpretations from an international perspective.* London: Kogan Page.

Phillips, J.C. (1997). Teaching offshore distance learners. In J. Osborne, D. Roberts, & J. Walker (Eds.), *Open, flexible and distance learning, 13th Biennial Forum of the Open and Distance Learning Association of Australia (ODLAA)* (pp. 369-373). Launceston: University of Tasmania.

Phillips, V. (1998). Virtual classrooms, real educations. *Nation's Business, 86*(5), 41-44.

Phipps, R. (1998). Quality assurance for distance learning in a global society. *International Higher Education, 13*(3). Retrieved May, 2005 from http://www.bc.edu/bc_org?avp/soe/cihe/newsletter/News13/text3.html

Phipps, R., & Merisotis, J. (1999). What's the difference? A review of contemporary research on the effectiveness of distance learning in higher education. Washington, DC: The Institute for Higher Education Policy. Retrieved March, 2003 from http://www.ihep.org/Pubs/PDF/Difference.pdf

Phipps, R., & Merisotis, J. (2000). Quality on the line: Benchmarks for success in internet-based distance education. Washington, DC: Institute for Higher Education Policy. Retrieved March, 2003 from http://www.ihep.com/quality.pdf

Pincas, A. (2001). Culture, cognition and communication in global education. *Distance Education, 22*(1), 30-51.

Ponzurick, T.G., France, K., & Logar, C.M. (2000). Delivering graduate marketing education: An analysis of face-to-face versus distance education. *Journal of Marketing Education, 22*(3), 180-187.

Pratt, D. (1994). *Curriculum planning: A handbook for professionals*. Orlando, FL: Harcourt Brace.

Race, P. (1994). *The open learning handbook*. 2nd Edition. London: Kogan Page.

Ragan, L.C. (1999). Good teaching is good teaching: An emerging set of guiding principles and practices for the design and development of distance education. *Cause/Effect, 22*(1), 20-24. Retrieved August, 2005 from http://www.educause.edu/ir/library/html/cem/cem99/cem9915.html

Ricketts, J.C., Irani, T., & Jones, L. (2003). The effect of instructional delivery methods on the critical thinking disposition of distance learners and traditional on-campus learners. *Journal of Southern Agricultural Education Research, 53*(1), 59-71. Retrieved November, 2003 from http://pubs.aged.tamu.edu/jsaer/pdf/Vol53/53-03-059.pdf

Riffee, W.R. (2003). Putting a face on distance education programs. *Syllabus*, February, 2003, 10-13. Retrieved March, 2006 from http://www.campus-technology.com/article.asp?id=7233

Rizvi, F., (2004). Offshore Australian higher education. International higher education, *1*(3). Retrieved November, 2005 from http://www.bc.edu/bc_org/avp/soe/cihe/newsletter/News37/text004.htm

Roblyer, M.D., & Wiencke, W. (2003). Design and use of a rubric to assess and encourage interactive qualities in distance courses. *The American Journal of Distance Education, 17*(2), 77-98.

Romiszowski, A. (1993). *Telecommunications and distance education*. Syracuse, N.Y.: ERIC Digest, ERIC Clearinghouse on Information Resources. (ERIC Document Reproduction Service No. ED 358 841). Retrieved May, 2003 from http://www.ericdigests.org/1993/distance.htm

Ross, L.R., & Powell, R. (1990). Relationships between gender and success in distance education courses: A preliminary investigation. *Research in Distance Education, 2*(2), 10-11.

Rovai, A.P., & Barnum, K.T. (2003). On-line course effectiveness: An analysis of student interactions and perceptions of learning. *Journal of Distance Education, 18*(1), 57-73.

Rumble, G. (1986). *The planning and management of distance education.* London: Croom Helm.

Ryan, Y. (2002). Emerging indicators of success and failure in borderless higher education. *Observatory on Borderless Higher Education.* Retrieved March, 2006 from http://www.obhe.ac.uk/products/reports/pdf/February2002.pdf

Saba, F. (2000). Research in distance education: A status report. *International Review of Research in Open and Distance Learning, 1*(1). Retrieved September 2005 from http://www.irrodl.org/content/v1.1/farhad.pdf

Sanchez, A. (1994). Trends and opportunities: Community colleges will need to "re-engineer" their organizations. *Community College Times, 6*(14), 2.

Schauer, J., Rockwell, S.K., Fritz, S., & Marx, D. (1998). *Education, assistance, and support needed for distance delivery: Faculty and administration perceptions.* Paper presented at the Annual Conference on Distance Teaching, Madison, WI. (ERIC Document Reproduction Service No. ED 422 871).

Schoorman, D. (2000). What really do we mean by internationalization. *Contemporary Education, 71*(4), 5-11.

Schweb, C., Kelley, K.B., & Orr, G.J. (1998). *Training and retaining faculty for online courses: Challenges and strategies.* Paper presented at the Annual Conference on Distance Teaching, Madison, WI. (ERIC Document Reproduction Service No. ED 422 874).

Seliger, H.W., & Shohamy, E. (2000). *Second language research methods.* Oxford, England: Oxford University Press.

Setaro, J. (2000). How E-learning can increase ROI for training. Retrieved July, 2003 from http://www.learning.thinq.com/

Sherron, G., & Boettcher, J. (1997). *Distance learning: The shift to interactivity.* CAUSE Professional Paper Series #17. Boulder, CO: CAUSE. Retrieved November, 2005 from http://www.educause.edu/ir/library/pdf/PUB3017.pdf

Sherry, L. (1996). Issues in distance learning. *International Journal of Educational Telecommunications, 1*(4), 337-365. Retrieved May 2003 from http://carbon.cudenver.edu/~lsherry/pubs/issues.html

Shin, N. (2003). Transactional presence as a critical predictor of success in distance learning. *Distance Education, 24*(1), 69-86.

Sigala, M. (2004). The evolution of internet pedagogy: Benefits for tourism and hospitality education. *Journal of Hospitality, Leisure, Sport and Tourism Education, 1*(2). Retrieved March 2006 from http://www.hlst.heacademy.ac.uk/Johlste/vol1no2/academic/0004.html

168

Simonson, M., Smaldino, S., Albright, M., & Zvacek, S. (2000). *Teaching and learning at a distance: Foundations of distance education.* Upper Saddle River, New York: Prentice Hall.

Simpson, O. (2000). *Supporting students in open and distance learning.* London: Kogan Page.

Simon, H.A. (1994). Interview. *OMNI Magazine, 16*(9), 71-89.

Singh, M., & Han, J. (2005). Globalizing flexible work in universities: Socio-technical dilemmas in internationalizing education. *International Review of Research in Open and Distance Learning, 6*(1). Retrieved March 2006 from: http://www.irrodl.org/content/v6.1/singh_han.html

Smith, P.L., & Dillon, C.L. (1999). Comparing distance learning and classroom learning: Conceptual considerations. *American Journal of Distance Education, 13*(2), 6-23.

Sonner, B.S. (1999). Success in the capstone business course—assessing the effectiveness of distance learning. *Journal of Education for Business, 74*(4), 243-247.

Spooner, F., Jordan, L., Algozzine, B., & Spooner, M. (1999). Student ratings of instruction in distance learning and on-campus classes. *Journal of Educational Research, 92*(3), 132-140. Retrieved September, 2004 from http://www.umsl.edu/technology/frc/pdfs/student%20ratings%20DL%20and%20on_campus.pdf

Stark, S., & Warne, T. (1999). Connecting the distance: Relational issues for participants in a distance learning programme. *Journal of Further and Higher Education, 23*(3), 391-402.

Stein, D. (1998). *Situated learning in adult education.* (ERIC Document Reproduction Service No. ED418250). Columbus OH: ERIC Clearinghouse on Adult Career and Vocational Education.

St.Pierre, S., & Olson, L.K. (1991). Student perspectives on the effectiveness of correspondence instruction. *The American Journal of Distance Education, 5*(3), 65-71.

Summers, J. (1991). Effect of interactivity upon student achievement completion intervals and affective perceptions. *Journal of Educational Technology Systems, 19*(1), 53-57.

Swan, K. (2001). Virtual interaction: Design factors affecting student satisfaction and perceived learning in asynchronous online courses. *Distance Education, 22*(2), 306-331.

Sweeney, J. (1995). *Vision 2020: Evaluation report.* Ames, IA: Research Institute for Studies in Education.

Tait, A., & Mills, R. (2001). Introduction: Supporting the student in open and distance learning. *Proceedings of the 9th Cambridge international conference on open and distance learning.* Cambridge, England.

Tallman, F.D. (1994). Satisfaction and completion in correspondence study: The influence of instructional and student-support services. *The American Journal of Distance Education, 8*(2), 43-57.

Taylor, J. C. (2000). *New millennium distance education.* Presentation. Retrieved March, 2004 from http://www.usq.edu.au/users/taylorj/publications_presentations/2000IGNOU.doc

Taylor, J. C. (2001). *Fifth generation distance education*. Higher education series: Report No.40 June
2001. DETYA: Canberra. Retrieved March, 2004 from
http://www.dest.gov.au/archive/highered/hes/hes40/hes40.pdf

Taylor, S., & Paton, R. (2002). Corporate universities. Historical development, conceptual analysis and
relations with public sector higher education. Report. *Observatory on Borderless Higher
Education*, London, UK. Retrieved January, 2006 from
http://www.obhe.ac.uk/products/reports/pdf/July2002.pdf

Terry, N. (2001.) Assessing enrollment and attrition rates for the online MBA. *T H E Journal
(Technological Horizons in Education)*, *28*(7), 64-68.

Thompson, M.M. (1998). Distance learners in higher education. In C.C. Gibson, (Eds.), *Distance learners
in higher education: Institutional responses for quality outcomes* (pp. 9-23). Madison, WI:
Atwood Publishing.

Thorpe, M. (2003). Continual reinvention: The future for open and distance learning. Keynote
presentation at the *10th Cambridge international conference in open and distance education*,
Cambridge, September 2003. Retrieved August, 2005 from
http://kn.open.ac.uk/public/document.cfm?docid=4195

Threlkeld, R., & Brzoska, K. (1994). Research in distance education. In B. Willis (Ed.), *Distance
education: Strategies and tools* (pp. 41-66). Englewood Cliffs, NJ: Educational Technology
Publications.

Tomasic, R. (2002). Guanxi and sustainable teaching and research programs in business and law in the
People's Republic of China. *In Proceedings of the 16th Australian international education
conference*, Hobart, 2-4 October 2002. Retrieved February, 2005 from:
www.businessandlaw.vu.edu.au/cicgr/Tomasic_p.pdf

Trilling, B., & Hood, P. (1999). Learning, technology, and education reform in the knowledge age or
"We're wired, webbed, and windowed. Now what?" *Educational Technology, 39*(3), 5-18.

UNESCO (2000). Distance education for the information society: Policies, pedagogy and professional
development. Moscow: UNESCO-IITE. Retrieved February, 2006 from http://kenya-
seminar.iite.ru/docs/Analyt_Survey.pdf

UNESCO & Council of Europe. (2001). Code of good practice in the provision of transnational
education. Bucharest: UNESCO-CEPES. Retrieved June 2002, from
http://www.cepes.ro/hed/recogn/groups/transnat/code.htm

U.S. Department of Education, National Center for Education Statistics (1999). *Distance education at
postsecondary education institutions: 1997-98*. NCES 2000-013. L. Lewis, K. Snow, E. Farris, &
D. Levin (Eds.). Washington, DC. Retrieved November, 2005 from
http://nces.ed.gov/pubs2000/2000013.pdf

Valentine, D. (2002). Distance learning: Promises, problems, and possibilities. *Journal of Distance Learning Administration, 5*(3). Retrieved May, 2004 from http://www.westga.edu/%7Edistance/ojdla/fall53/valentine53.html

Van Damme, D. (2001). Higher education in the age of globalisation: The need for a new regulatory framework for recognition, quality assurance and accreditation. Introductory Paper for the UNESCO Expert Meeting, Paris, 10-11 September 2001. Retrieved September, 2005 from http://www.unesco.org/education/studyingabroad/highlights/global_forum/presentations/keynote_eng.doc

Van den Brande, L. (1992). *Flexible and distance learning.* West Sussex, UK: Wiley.

van der Vende, M.C. (2003). Globalisation and access to higher education. *Journal of Studies in International Education, 7*(2), 193-206.

Verduin, J. R., II, & Clark, T. A. (1991). *Distance education: The foundations of effective practice.* San Francisco: Jossey-Bass.

Vignoli, G. (2004). What is transnational education? Online document. Retrieved March, 2005 from http://www.cimea.it/servlets/resources?contentId=2831&resourceName=Inserisci%20allegato

Visser, L. (1998). *The development of motivational communication in distance education support.* University of Twente, Enschede, Netherlands.

Wagner, E.D. (1994). In support of a functional definition of interaction. *The American Journal of Distance Education, 8*(2), 6-29.

Walker, S. (2005). Keynote address: Education Sector Response. *CEDA conference, lifelong learning: Challenges of an ageing workforce.* Retrieved March, 2006 from http://www.deakin.edu.au/vc/presentations/CEDA-presentation-11.pdf

Watkins, B.L. (1991). A quite radical idea: The invention and elaboration of collegiate correspondence study. In B.L. Watkins & S.J. Wright (Eds), *The foundations of American distance education* (pp. 1-35). Dubuque, Iowa: Kendall/Hunt.

Weber, J. (1996). *The compressed video experience.* Paper presented at Summer Conference of the Association of Small Computer Users. North Myrtle Beach, South Carolina. (ERIC Document Reproduction Service No. ED 405 838).

Welch, A. (2002). Going global? Internationalizing Australian universities in a time of global crisis. *Comparative Education Review, 46*(4), 433-473.

Weinstein, P. (1997). Education goes the distance: Overview. *Technology & Learning, 17*(8), 24-25.

Wenger, E. (1998). *Communities of practice: Learning, meaning, and identity.* Cambridge, UK: Cambridge University Press.

Wilkes, C.W., & Burnham, B.R. (1991). Adult learner motivations and electronics distance education. *The American Journal of Distance Education, 5*(1), 43-50.

Willis, B. (1995). Distance education: An overview. College of Engineering, University of Idaho. Retrieved January, 2003 from http://www.edutec.net/Textos/Alia/WILLIS/dist1.htm

Wilson, L., & Vlăsceanu, L. (2000). Transnational education and the recognition of qualifications. In *Internationalization of higher education: An institutional perspective*, Bucharest, UNESCO-CEPES Papers on Higher Education, 75-85.

Wisher, R. A., & Curnow, C. K. (1998). *Techniques for evaluating distance learning events.* Proceedings of the annual conference on distance teaching & learning. (ERIC Document Reproduction Service No. ED422887).

Wolcott, L. (1996). Distant, but not distanced: A learner-centered approach to distance education. *TechTrends, 41*(5), 23-27.

Woodley, A., & Kirkwood, A. (1986). *Evaluation in distance learning.* Paper 10. Resources in Education. (ERIC Document Reproduction Service No. ED 304 122).

Wyatt, S. (2001). Crossing the boundaries: Overcoming borders and understanding languages. *Western Cooperative of Educational Telecommunications (WCET) 13th Annual Conference.* Coeur d'Alene, Idaho, Oct 2001. Retrieved November, 2002 from http://www.wiche.edu/telecom/events/conference/2001/Presentations/Scott%20Wyatt.ppt

Xenos,M., Pierrakeas, C., & Pintelas, P. (2002). A survey on student dropout causes concerning the students in the course of Informatics of the Hellenic Open University. *Computers & Education, 39*, 361–377. Retrieved September 2005 from http://quality.eap.gr/Publications/XM/Chapters-Journals/J04%20-%20Student%20Dropout%20Rates%20(pre-p).pdf

Yuen, K.S., Timmers, S., & Chau, H. (1993). Distance education in an urban environment: experience of the Open Learning Institute of Hong Kong. In B. Scriven, R. Lundin, & Y. Ryan (Eds.) *Distance education for the twenty-first century*, (pp. 130-133). Brisbane, Australia: QUT.

Zhao, Y., Lei, J., Yan, B., Lai, C., & Tan, H.S. (2005). What makes the difference? A practical analysis of research on the effectiveness of distance education. *Teachers College Record, 107*(8), 1836-1884.

Ziguras, C. (2000). *New frontiers, new technologies, new pedagogies. Educational technology and the internationalisation of higher education in South East Asia.* Monash Centre for Research in International Education: Melbourne.

Ziguras, C. (2002). *Education beyond our shores: Defining the way forward.* Workshop report. International Policy & Development Unit, Strategic Information and Resourcing Division, New Zealand Ministry of Education. October 2002. Retrieved September, 2004 from http://www.minedu.govt.nz/web/downloadable/dl7382_v1/workshop-report-final.doc

APPENDIX A

Survey

Survey for Students of Offshore Degree Program – Section A

Please rate the following characteristics of this course as quickly and honestly as possible. For each item, simply **circle** the number that best represents your attitude or opinion.

Instruction/Instructor Characteristics

		Very Poor	Poor	Average	Good	Very Good
1.	The clarity with which course objectives, requirements, and assignments were communicated.	1	2	3	4	5
2.	The time given in classes to copy down the presented lecture material.	1	2	3	4	5
3.	The production quality of the lecture presentations.	1	2	3	4	5
4.	The extent to which lecture presentations relied on electronic media.	1	2	3	4	5
5.	The degree to which lecture notes and presentations helped you better understand the course material.	1	2	3	4	5
6.	The time within which tests and written assignments were marked and returned.	1	2	3	4	5
7.	The extent to which electronic media were used for assignment submission and feedback.	1	2	3	4	5
8.	The degree to which instructional techniques that were used to teach the classes (e.g. demonstrations, group discussions, case studies, etc.) helped you better understand the course material.	1	2	3	4	5
9.	The extent to which classrooms were free of distractions (e.g., noise from adjacent rooms, people coming in and out, other students talking with each other, etc.)	1	2	3	4	5
10.	The extent to which instructors made the students feel that they were part of the class.	1	2	3	4	5
11.	The instructors' communication skills.	1	2	3	4	5
12a.	The University instructors' organisation and preparation for classes.	1	2	3	4	5
12b.	The Hong Kong instructors' organisation and preparation for classes.	1	2	3	4	5
13a.	The University instructors' dedication to students and teaching.	1	2	3	4	5
13b.	The Hong Kong instructors' dedication to students and teaching.	1	2	3	4	5
14a.	The University instructors' teaching ability.	1	2	3	4	5
14b.	The Hong Kong instructors' teaching ability.	1	2	3	4	5
15a.	The extent to which the University instructors encouraged class participation.	1	2	3	4	5
15b.	The extent to which the Hong Kong instructors encouraged class participation.	1	2	3	4	5
16a.	The telephone/email accessibility of the University instructors outside of classes.	1	2	3	4	5
16b.	The telephone/email accessibility of the Hong Kong instructors outside of classes.	1	2	3	4	5

		Very Poor	Poor	Average	Good	Very Good
17.	The degree to which instructors encouraged communication between students, and between students and instructors.	1	2	3	4	5
18.	The extent to which the course material was sufficient to support study at home (independent of class).	1	2	3	4	5
19a.	Overall, the University instructors were:	1	2	3	4	5
19b.	Overall, the Hong Kong instructors were:	1	2	3	4	5

Technological Characteristics

		Very Poor	Poor	Average	Good	Very Good
20.	The quality of the technology used in classes.	1	2	3	4	5
21.	The ease of use of technology.	1	2	3	4	5
22.	The extent to which the course relied on the use of technology in the classroom or the college.	1	2	3	4	5
23.	The extent to which the course relied on the use of technology at home.	1	2	3	4	5
24.	The degree of confidence you had that classes would not be interrupted or cancelled due to technical problems.	1	2	3	4	5
25.	The quality of technical support provided.	1	2	3	4	5
26.	The overall usefulness of course Web sites.	1	2	3	4	5

Course Management and Coordination

		Very Poor	Poor	Average	Good	Very Good
27.	The present means of exchanging course material between you and the instructors.	1	2	3	4	5
28.	Your ability to access the university library and other student resources.	1	2	3	4	5
29.	Your ability to access a computer when, and if, needed.	1	2	3	4	5
30.	The general attitude of the administrative/technical staff, e.g. in delivering materials, maintaining classrooms.	1	2	3	4	5
31.	The accessibility of administrative/technical staff.	1	2	3	4	5
32.	The promptness with which course materials were delivered.	1	2	3	4	5
33.	Your ability to access the university course coordinator when needed.	1	2	3	4	5
34.	Class enrollment and registration procedures.	1	2	3	4	5
35.	Your opportunity to evaluate the course.	1	2	3	4	5
36.	The extent to which, in your opinion, the university responds to evaluations.	1	2	3	4	5
37.	The degree of organisational support.	1	2	3	4	5

38. The BSc in Computer Science course is effective. ☐ YES ☐ NO (Check one)
   Why?

39. Would you participate in a similar course in the future? ☐ YES ☐ NO (Check one)
   Why?

Section B

In each category, please rank only the top THREE characteristics that, in your opinion, contribute to the effectiveness of the course. Number the characteristics in order of importance (1=most important).

1. Category: Student (Rank only top three).

Rank	Characteristics
	Works as a team player.
	Has positive attitude towards technology-based learning.
	Is motivated and self-disciplined.
	Is confident in using technology.
	Knows how to work independently.
	Is involved and participates.
	Is willing to ask instructors for assistance.

2. Category: University Instructor and Learning Environment (Rank only top three).

Rank	Characteristics
	Understands course requirements, students' characteristics and needs.
	Encourages students to take responsibility for their own learning.
	Encourages communication between students, and students and instructors.
	Demonstrates dedication to course, teaching and students.
	Uses effective communication skills.
	Conducts students' needs assessment and course evaluation.
	Ensures students' support services.

3. Category: Hong Kong Instructor and Learning Environment (Rank only top three).

Rank	Characteristics
	Understands course requirements, students' characteristics and needs.
	Encourages students to take responsibility for their own learning.
	Encourages communication between students, and students and instructors.
	Demonstrates dedication to course, teaching and students.
	Uses effective communication skills.
	Conducts students' needs assessment and course evaluation.
	Ensures students' support services.

4. Category: University Instructor – Technology and Organisation (Rank only top three).

Rank	Characteristics
	Has positive attitude towards technology.
	Demonstrates control over technology.
	Adapts course materials for delivery through electronic media.
	Has experience with technology-based courses.
	Is well prepared and organised.
	Is proficient in instructional design.
	Uses interactive instructional strategies.
	Provides well-designed syllabus and presentation outlines.
	Develops effective graphics.

5. Category: Hong Kong Instructor – Technology and Organisation (Rank only top three).

Rank	Characteristics
	Has positive attitude towards technology.
	Demonstrates control over technology.
	Adapts course materials for delivery through electronic media.
	Has experience with technology-based courses.
	Is well prepared and organised.
	Is proficient in instructional design.
	Uses interactive instructional strategies.
	Provides well-designed syllabus and presentation outlines.
	Develops effective graphics.

6. Category: Curriculum and Instruction Design (Rank only top three).

Rank	Characteristics
	Relates the new material to previous student knowledge.
	Integrates all course elements into a well-paced package.
	Is relevant to job/career.
	Creates logical sequences for each element presented.
	Course objectives and learning outcomes are communicated to students.
	Instructors and students agree on deadlines for completion and marking of assignments.
	Learning objectives are supported by instructional methodologies.

7. Category: Interaction (Rank only top three).

Rank	Characteristics
	Timely feedback on assignments and projects.
	Involvement in small learning groups.
	Use of interactive instructional strategies.
	Frequent contact with the instructor.
	Use of electronic media and telephone to interact with instructors.
	Development of formats and strategies encouraging communication between students, and students and instructors.

8. Category: Evaluation and Assessment (Rank only top three).

Rank	Characteristics
	Assessment of students' attitudes and levels of satisfaction.
	Assessment of the relevance of course content in practice.
	Methods of assessment match learning objectives.
	Continuous evaluation of students' academic progress.
	Continuous evaluation of the course.

9. Category: Technology (Rank only top three).

Rank	Characteristics
	Current products are used.
	Is helpful and easy to use.
	Is available and reliable.
	Software applications are appropriate and easy to use.
	Access to technical assistance throughout the course.

10. Category: Course Management and Organisational Support (Rank only top three).

Rank	Characteristics
	Timely preparation of course materials.
	Procedures exist to quickly respond to student complaints.
	Institution ensures high quality of the course.
	Student support services are provided (e.g. student registration, distribution of materials, ordering of textbooks, processing of examination results).
	Training on obtaining information through course Web sites, electronic databases, interlibrary loans, etc. provided.
	Effective overall course coordination.

11. What was your reason for enrolling in this course?

12. Is this type of course (offered by an offshore university) worthwhile? Why?

13. Would you prefer the course to be offered fully online?

APPENDIX B

Survey cover sheet

Victoria University of Technology

Critical Success Characteristics in Offshore Computing Programs

Information to Participants of the Research Study

We would like to invite you to be a part of a study into critical success characteristics of offshore computing programs conducted by Victoria University researchers Dr John Horwood and Iwona Miliszewska.

As a student of an Australian University degree program, you have many experiences and insights that are important in the study of offshore programs. The attached questionnaire is designed to capture your knowledge in this area. Firstly you will be asked to indicate your level of satisfaction with the current program; secondly, identify critical success factors of offshore programs; and finally, rank the importance of the identified factors. The information collected will allow an in-depth examination of the content, structure and process of the programs.

The attached questionnaire is one component of data being collected for the study on the critical success characteristics of offshore computing programs. Your participation is strictly voluntary. Your responses will be anonymous and results will not be released in any identifiable form.

Procedures:
If you are willing to participate, please complete the questionnaire and return it in the enclosed envelope to the collection box. The questionnaire should take approximately twenty minutes to complete. Please complete all sections printed on each page.

Any queries about your participation in this project may be directed to the researcher (Name: Iwona Miliszewska, ph. +613 9688 4094, email: Iwona.Miliszewska@vu.edu.au). If you have any queries or complaints about the way you have been treated, you may contact the Secretary, University Human Research Ethics Committee, Victoria University of Technology, PO Box 14428 MC, Melbourne, 8001 (telephone no: +613-9688 4710).

APPENDIX C

Group interviews guide

Group Interviews Guide

Introduction – researcher introduces herself and explains the purpose of the group interview:

"This group interview is part of a doctoral study looking at ways in which various aspects of offshore education impact on a particular offshore computing program, e.g. the use of technology, organisational support, etc. In this case, the program is X (Y, Z). We will spend an hour together discussing a number of questions and sharing opinions with the participants of this group. Please be assured that neither you nor your answers will be identifiable. All the information gathered in this study will be reported collectively and it will not be revealed what individual participants have said. Please note, that in order to reduce the possibility of any type of bias, I am not going to facilitate the group, and there is one additional note taker beside myself. The notes will only be shared between the note taker, the facilitator and myself. The purpose of the notes is to help analyse the discussion."

Researcher introduces facilitator and note taker. The facilitator then asks participants to introduce themselves.

Warm up question: What made you decide to enrol in the program?

Key content questions:
1. What do you find exciting about the program?
2. What reservations or fears did you have when considering the program?
3. What is it like to be a student in this program?
4. To what extent does the program meet your expectations?
5. Which aspects of the program, if any, would you like enhanced?
6. Which aspects of the program, if any, would you like reduced?
7. Would you prefer the course to be fully online, or face-to-face, why?

Summary
1. Is this offshore education experience worthwhile?
2. What advice about this program would you give to the Australian university offering it?

Closing remarks:
Thank everyone for their participation and remind them that nothing they said during the group meeting will identify a particular person.

APPENDIX D

Information to participants of group interviews

Victoria University of Technology

Critical Success Characteristics in Offshore Computing Programs

Information to Participants of Group Interviews

We would like to invite you to be a part of a study into critical success characteristics of offshore computing programs conducted by Victoria University researchers Dr John Horwood and Iwona Miliszewska.

As a student of an Australian University degree program, you have many experiences and insights that are important in the study of offshore programs.

You will be asked to participate in a group interview (approximately one hour long) with other students in which you will be asked to talk about your experiences and opinions about the offshore computing course in which you are enrolled. Specifically, you will be asked to discuss reasons for enrolling in the course, aspects of the course that you like most, and aspects that could be improved and suggestions of possible improvements.

We do not expect any risks from participating in the study. Please note, that during the discussion, you do not have to answer any questions that you do not wish to answer. You will also be free to leave the group at any time. You may also ask questions about research procedures at any time and these questions will be answered. You may direct further questions to the researcher (refer to the contact details provided at the bottom of this page).

Detailed notes of the discussion will be taken to maintain the accuracy of your statements. The information that you give us will be confidential. To protect your identity, you will not be identified personally in any way. The notes will be kept under lock and key until the completion of data analysis with only Dr John Horwood and Iwona Miliszewska able to access them. Upon completion of the analysis tapes will be destroyed.

The notes will be coded for themes in the comments. It is possible that specific comments will be reported in relation to a particular theme. Real names will not be tied to these comments. If, at any point, you are concerned about a comment that you have made, please contact the researcher, Iwona Miliszewska, and your comments will be erased from all records if you so choose. In the event of publication of this research, no personally identifying information will be disclosed.

Any queries about your participation in this project may be directed to the researcher (Name: Iwona Miliszewska, ph. +613 9688 4094, email: Iwona.Miliszewska@vu.edu.au). If you have any queries or complaints about the way you have been treated, you may contact the Secretary, University Human Research Ethics Committee, Victoria University of Technology, PO Box 14428 MC, Melbourne, 8001 (telephone no: +613-9688 4710).

APPENDIX E

Consent form for group interview

Victoria University of Technology

Consent Form for Group Interview

INFORMATION TO PARTICIPANTS:

The group interview in which you will be participating is part of a research study examining ways in which various aspects of offshore education, e.g. the use of technology, organisational support, etc., impact on offshore computing programs.

Your participation in the group interview is strictly voluntary and anonymous. Neither you nor your answers will be identifiable in any way, and all the information gathered in this study will be reported collectively.

CERTIFICATION BY PARTICIPANT

I,

of

certify that I am at least 18 years old and that I am voluntarily giving my consent to participate in the scientific investigation entitled: **Critical Success Characteristics in Offshore Computing Programs** being conducted at Victoria University of Technology by: **Dr John Horwood and Iwona Miliszewska**.

I certify that the objectives of the investigation, together with any risks to me associated with the procedures listed hereunder to be carried out in the experiment, have been fully explained to me by: **Dr John Horwood and Iwona Miliszewska**, and that I freely consent to participation involving the use on me of these procedures.

Procedures:
The research study will be briefly described, and participants of the group interview introduced. The investigators will set ground rules and expectations for group members of mutual respect and courtesy. The interview session will last approximately an hour. During the session you will discuss, together with other group participants, questions relevant to the study. You do not have to answer any questions that you do not wish to answer. You will also be free to leave the group at any time. You may also ask questions about research procedures at any time and these questions will be answered.

I certify that I have had the opportunity to have any questions answered and that I understand that I can withdraw from this investigation at any time and that this withdrawal will not jeopardise me in any way.

I have been informed that the information I provide will be kept confidential.

Signed: ....

Witness other than the experimenter: **Date:** ....

....

Any queries about your participation in this project may be directed to the researcher (Name: Iwona Miliszewska, ph. +613 9688 4094, email: Iwona.Miliszewska@vu.edu.au). If you have any queries or complaints about the way you have been treated, you may contact the Secretary, University Human Research Ethics Committee, Victoria University of Technology, PO Box 14428 MC, Melbourne, 8001 (telephone no: +613-9688 4710).

APPENDIX F

Ethics application approval letter

Victoria University of Technology

PO Box 14428
Melbourne City
MC 8001 Australia

Telephone:
(03) 9688 4000
Facsimile:
(03) 9689 4069

Footscray Park Campus
Ballarat Road
Footscray

MEMORANDUM

TO: Dr John Horwood
             School of Computer Science and Mathematics

FROM: Dr Alan Hayes
             Chair, Human Research Ethics Committee
             Faculty of Science, Engineering and Technology

DATE: 28 November, 2003

SUBJECT: **HRETH.ES 12/02 Critical success characteristics in
                 offshore computing programs**

At its meeting of the 25 November, 2003 the Faculty of Science, Engineering and Technology Human Research Ethics Committee confirmed that your application

Critical success characteristics in offshore computing programs

has been **approved** until December 1, 2004.

You are reminded that an annual report (form can be downloaded from the Office for Research webpage) must be submitted within a year of approval or at the completion of the study, whichever comes first.

If you have any questions or queries about the requirements of the Committee's deliberations please do not hesitate to contact me via e-mail or on 9688 4658.

Sincerely,

Dr Alan Hayes
Chair, Human Research Committee
Faculty of Science, Engineering and Technology

VDM publishing house ltd.

Scientific Publishing House

offers

free of charge publication

of current academic research papers, Bachelor´s Theses, Master's Theses, Dissertations or Scientific Monographs

If you have written a thesis which satisfies high content as well as formal demands, and you are interested in a remunerated publication of your work, please send an e-mail with some initial information about yourself and your work to *info@vdm-publishing-house.com.*

Our editorial office will get in touch with you shortly.

VDM Publishing House Ltd.
Meldrum Court 17.
Beau Bassin
Mauritius
www.vdm-publishing-house.com

www.ingramcontent.com/pod-product-compliance
Lightning Source LLC
LaVergne TN
LVHW042334060326
832902LV00006B/170